Best 100 Juices for Kids

Best 100 Juices for Kids

Totally Yummy,
Awesomely Healthy,
& Naturally Sweetened
Homemade Alternatives
to Soda Pop, Sports
Drinks, & Expensive
Bottled Juices

Jessica Fisher

THE HARVARD COMMON PRESS
BOSTON, MASSACHUSETTS

The Harvard Common Press
www.harvardcommonpress.com

Printed in China
Printed on acid-free paper

Library of Congress Cataloging-in-Publication Data
Fisher, Jessica Getskow.
    Best 100 juices for kids : totally yummy, awesomely healthy, & naturally sweetened homemade alternatives to soda pop, sports drinks, and expensive bottled juices / Jessica Getskow Fisher.
        pages cm
      ISBN 978-1-55832-829-7 (pbk.)
      1. Juicers. 2. Fruit juices. 3. Smoothies (Beverages) 4. Children--Nutrition. I. Title.
      TX840.J84F78 2014
      641.3'4--dc23
                                    2013036546

Special bulk-order discounts are available on this and other Harvard Common Press books. Companies and organizations may purchase books for premiums or resale, or may arrange a custom edition, by contacting the Marketing Director at the web address above.

Front cover and interior photographs by Dimitris66/iStockphoto
Recipe photographs by Brian Samuels
Author photographs by Sharon Leppellere

10 9 8 7 6 5 4 3 2 1

To N, J, C, J, C, and E:
my six sweet children, who have given
my life more joy and meaning than
I could ever have dreamed possible.
I love you to the moon and back.

Contents

Introduction

Kids love sweet drinks. Juices, sodas, and sports drinks—they all offer cool refreshment on a hot day or after the big game. They bring comfort when a cold or flu strikes. They make great accompaniments to pizza on a Friday night.

In a word, they're just plain *fun*!

They can also be laden with sugar, artificial colors, and artificial flavorings. I know, leave it to a mom to be the bearer of bad news. But many of the beverages marketed to kids are just plain junk.

Rather than be a killjoy, though, I choose to be a "Yes Mom." I want to say "Yes!" when my kids ask for something sweet and refreshing on a hot summer day. I want to say "Yes!" and celebrate a hockey goal with a chilled bottle of lemon-lime sports drink. I want to say "Yes!" to ginger ale on our family pizza night.

I can do all that by preparing and serving homemade juices, sodas, and sports drinks.

Making homemade juice is a fun and creative alternative to purchasing commercially made versions. Sending fruit, juice, and crushed ice through the blender produces a frosty smoothie that can rival the local juice bar's selection. Mixing a bit of sea salt with water, juice, and honey creates a homemade sports ade that beats the bottle. Blending mint and honey syrup with juice and soda water creates a sparkling beverage to please kids of all ages.

With the great variety and quality of fresh produce available to us today, there's no reason not to whip up homemade juices, smoothies, sodas, and sports drinks. You can say "Yes!" and provide a healthier alternative to your kids at the same time.

Trust me. I'm a mom. I know these things.

Our Story

Years ago, I was a soda pop junkie. I drank a minimum of one soda every day. It was the thing that got me through the day: vanilla-flavored cola, served over crushed ice and savored through a straw.

During that season of life, I also gave birth to six children. And as children are apt to do, they all shared my love of fizzy sugar-laden drinks. (Well, except one. She likes her drinks flat.) I had a hard time telling them "No," knowing the wise child would inevitably reply, "But *you* drink it." I knew daily indulgence wasn't the best thing for my kids, but I compromised by allowing them a weekly soda binge over pizza as well as a few sips from my daily glass.

Eventually our family was hit with a few bad dental check-ups and a number of cavities to fill—mine as well as the children's. At about the same time, I started to do some in-depth food research about processed sugars, additives, and the American food supply as a whole. I realized then that I wasn't feeding my children (not to mention myself and my husband) the best possible food and drink. Without watching a single panic-inducing documentary, I simply concluded that we could be eating better.

Slowly, taking baby steps, I set out to reform our eating habits. I reduced our intake of processed foods, limited our fast food meals, and became intent on buying the best ingredients our budget could handle. My family's health became a bigger priority. Along the way, I ditched my soda-drinking habit and curbed theirs as well. (Coincidentally or not, our large dental bills have all but disappeared, too.)

Our new diet included more whole foods, more meals cooked from scratch, and more organic ingredients when we could afford them. Obviously, feeding six children isn't an inexpensive endeavor, but I decided to make every bite count. At this time, we also joined an organic produce co-op that delivered a ginormous box of fruits and vegetables each week. The weekly price of $36 for all the fruits and veggies we could eat was well worth it.

With the produce box came the opportunity to try a number of foods that I'd never purchased before—as well as some I'd never even heard of! My kids, my husband, and I were in for a new adventure. I wasn't following some faddish "eat-all-the-weird-things-you-can-eat" diet. I simply wanted to see what else the world had to offer in terms of good taste and nutrition. And I had an inkling that it didn't come in a brightly colored box or can marketed with a memorable jingle.

I'm happy to report that we've discovered the beauty of leeks, pea tendrils, pomegranates, and leafy greens. (We've also decided that we're happy to share our persimmons and collard greens with whatever friends and neighbors will take them off our hands.) While we still eat burgers and fries and pizza, and indulge in the occasional fountain drink, we enjoy more homemade whole foods, and our family's health is much better for it.

True to their roots and their mama's sweet tooth, my kids still crave a sweet drink. In the early years, we incorporated bottled juices and juice-based sparkling drinks into their pizza-night menu and let them enjoy the occasional smoothie-bar beverage or frozen juice pop. But all that glitters is not gold.

I started reading labels. *Ahem*. The labels on those bottles and frosty treats may boast of good nutrition, but these products often contain hidden sugars and additives that we'd be better off avoiding. I was stunned when I realized what was going into the blender at the local smoothie bar.

Enter the juice extractor, citrus press, blender, and ice pop molds.

In my efforts to have my sweet, tasty drinks and enjoy them with a clear conscience, too, I've taken my family to the next stage of the adventure: making these items at home.

A few small kitchen appliances are really all I need to make healthier versions of these special drinks my children crave. In the process, I also save money and introduce my kids to new tastes and flavors. Did you know that beets turn juice a beautiful shade of pink? And the produce-box parsnips that we once shunned work really well in homemade juices. Honey can be used in place of sugar in simple syrup, making a perfect natural sweetener for smoothies, slushies, and other cold drinks.

This book documents our family's journey down the road to creating homemade juices, smoothies, sports drinks, sparklies, slushies, and ice pops. I don't make any health claims. I'm a mom trying to feed her children well—and stay under budget. I don't know that drinking homemade juices will cure what ails us. I can't promise that your family's cavities will disappear, as ours seem to have done.

I do look at our homemade juices and other beverages as a fun part of our increasingly balanced and healthy diet. Kids love them. Adults do, too. Homemade juices are a great sweet treat we can enjoy daily; drinking them is a simple way to add some extra vitamins and minerals to our diet. They come in every color of the rainbow, without added colors, preservatives, or ingredients whose names you can't pronounce. And—speaking as a reformed soda junkie— that's something all moms and dads can celebrate.

Meet the Tasters

Once upon a time, I was a career woman with a master's degree and a leather satchel. I took a break from teaching public high school to have my brood of beautiful children 16 years ago, a decision I've never regretted. I've been honored to be their primary teacher and provide them with an at-home education.

Quite inadvertently, I re-entered the working world eight years ago, when I started writing for parenting magazines. My husband and children were a source of inspiration and encouragement to me. They continued as such later, when I began blogging at Life as Mom and Good Cheap Eats. For my first cookbook, *Not Your Mother's Make-Ahead and Freeze Cookbook (The Harvard Common Press, 2012),* they were my first and best taste testers and critics.

The same holds true for this book. Meet the tasters.

On the Web, I'm known as FishMama; my children are the FishKids. We called them this in real life, before I began blogging. Once the blogs started, we kept up their pseudonyms to give them some sense of privacy. After all, I was divulging everything else.

FishChick5 is the baby in a family of six children, clocking in at five years of age at this writing. She protests that she doesn't like a certain vegetable—until I tell her she loves it. Then she gobbles it down. May she always hold such simple trust in her mama! She loves anything pink, beet juice included.

FishChick7 is a helper and encourager. She loves to cook, offering her services to make homemade tortillas, peel shrimp, or juice up a bunch of fruit. Although she's a relatively good eater, appreciating the same "chick food" as her mother, she turns up her nose at cooked leafy greens.

FishBoy9 is my resident food critic and the youngest of my four sons. At age nine, he is quick to voice protest against squash and spinach. If a recipe passes muster with him, chances are good that anyone would enjoy it.

FishBoy11 is the third of the four brothers. He has a love of music, art, and culinary endeavors. While he will typically "eat anything," he does not hesitate to express his preferences. His culinary vocabulary and food descriptions can rival those of Alton Brown. One recent summer, he insisted that we learn how to make ravioli from scratch.

FishBoy13 has always been quick-witted, the keeper of odd knowledge. He is brilliance incarnate. He also prefers his food to be white or brown, although he is growing in his love of vegetables. He's not a fan of tomatoes, but he willingly downs all the recipes in this book, albeit issuing a reminder that the ones containing tomato aren't his favorites.

FishBoy16, my oldest, towers over both his parents. He has proven to be quite knowledgeable about health and nutrition. He gladly piles his plate high with spinach and other greens and sneaks all kinds of weird things into the protein drinks he mixes. He also hits a mean slap shot.

FishPapa, my main squeeze and confidant, is the glue that holds all this together. He puts up with all my wild and crazy schemes—and tries every juice and dish I hand him to taste. Well, almost.

The Basics of Home Juicing

Juices are the stuff of childhood memories. I can't open a bottle of commercial apple juice without being magically transported back to my preschool days, when our daily snack was a small paper cup of the stuff and a handful of animal crackers.

My grandmother had a collection of small juice glasses imprinted with images of Felix the Cat, Donald Duck, and Popeye, presumably from my mom's childhood. A glass of juice was a regular breakfast item whenever we visited her on summer trips to Minnesota.

But juice is not just for breakfast or snack time. When I lived in France, my French friends often offered a small glass of juice as part of the apéritif, or cocktail hour, accompanied by some olives or a handful of nuts to whet the appetite. And, yes, children were and are included in this nightly ritual.

My own children love juice with a passion. Over the years, I've limited their juice consumption because of concerns about price and nutrition. A lot of the "juices" on supermarket shelves are really "juice drinks," with added sugar and corn syrup. But unadulterated juices can run $4 to $5 a bottle—and you can imagine how quickly six kids go through a bottle!

I've found that homemade juices are, among other things, more filling than the bottled varieties, so a little can go a long way. I can also use great creativity in my choices of fruits and vegetables, introducing my kids to new flavors.

Serving sizes at our house vary, depending on the age of the child. The American Academy of Pediatrics recommends waiting until a child is one year old before serving him or her juice. For children between the ages of one and six, the AAP suggests limiting juice intake 4 to 6 ounces per day; the organization also advises that children ages seven to eighteen be limited to 8 to 12 ounces per day.

Most juice recipes in this book should make 15 to 20 ounces of juice. The amount may vary depending on the size of your produce and the quality of your juicer. Juicing is a very forgiving process. You can add fruits and vegetables until you get a result you like. Feel free to make substitutions if you don't have a particular item on hand. You might discover a new favorite!

Getting Started

When our family started on this journey of home juicing, I had limited knowledge about the process. I had grown up with my parents' backyard citrus trees, which produced more fruit than we could manage at one time. I learned about citrus juicing at a young age, freezing the juice in ice cube trays to be used throughout the year. As an adult, I experimented with juicing pomegranates, the most delectable but unwieldy of fruits, so that I could make pomegranate jelly, a favorite spread at our house.

Up until a few years ago, that was the extent of my juicing experience. Then one summer, when the weekly produce box yielded more peaches than we could possibly eat fresh, I started wondering about home juicing. I had a vague notion of what juicing was, based on television infomercials I'd seen as a teenager. Might a juicer be a good addition to our home?

That fall, I took the leap and picked up a bargain juicer at the local superstore. This adventure became a family affair as we tested different flavor combinations and learned what fruits and vegetables could be juiced successfully. Here's what we've learned.

What Can You Juice?

With a standard (centrifugal) juicer, you can juice almost any fruit or vegetable. You'll extract more juice from oranges, lemons, and the like by using a citrus press or citrus juicer. But you'll get a bit of extra goodness from the nutrients found in the peels and membranes of citrus fruits if you send them through a standard centrifugal juicer.

Most fruits and vegetables can be successfully juiced. Save bananas and avocados for smoothies, or process them separately in a blender and whisk them into the juice if you wish. Almost everything else is fair game, depending on how you prepare it and what type of juicer you have. See page 103 for a list of fruits and vegetables organized by season, so that you can maximize flavor and minimize cost when preparing juices at home.

Keep in mind that a sour peach will make a sour juice. It's best to use ripe, in-season fruit for best flavor. Consider this while you shop, and don't be afraid to ask the produce clerk for a sample. They are typically happy to let you try before you buy. The same holds true for most farmers' markets and produce stands.

What's the Difference Between a Smoothie and a Juice?

Most of us know about smoothies, which are blended drinks made from fruits, juices, ice, and oftentimes a dairy component, like milk or yogurt; for a more dessert-like treat, frozen yogurt or sherbet can be used. A smoothie retains all the fiber of whatever fruits or vegetables it contains. A juice, however, is the liquid extracted from those ingredients, typically with much of the fiber removed. Both can be beneficial, and nutritionists debate which is most healthful. Those who favor juices claim that the lack of fiber allows nutrients to be absorbed better and more quickly into the body, while smoothie enthusiasts emphasize the importance of fiber for healthy digestion. But there's no need to limit yourself to one or the other: My kids and I know that both juices and smoothies are tasty and full of good stuff.

What Equipment Do You Need?

To make homemade juices and smoothies, you really need just two small kitchen appliances: a juicing machine for juices and a blender for smoothies. If you're not sure you want to make the investment, ask a friend or relative if you might borrow his or her machine for a week or so to give it a spin. By test-driving the appliance, you can see if it's a purchase you'd like to make.

Although some of the recipes in this book can be made without a juicer—a.k.a. a juice extractor—most do require that appliance. The juice recipes here were tested with centrifugal juicers from both the low and the middle price ranges.

Juicers

There are several types of juicers to choose from. To select the best one for you, factor in your family size, how often you plan to juice, and what items you want to juice. A good way to start, as I mentioned, is to borrow a juicer from a friend and see whether you like that type. Otherwise, begin with a small, inexpensive juicer and work yourself up to a bigger, badder machine as you see the need. We started with the least expensive juicer we could find, and it did a great job for our purposes at the outset. Later, as we became more committed to juicing, we switched to a higher-end model, which I found easier to assemble and clean and which did a more thorough job of extracting juice.

Always comparison shop and check thrift stores. There are plenty of folks out there who thought they would become juice masters and never even took the machine out of the box. You might find a good deal, thanks to those impulse shoppers.

CITRUS JUICERS

Citrus juicers are the least expensive juicing machines. A citrus juicer, reamer, or press is used solely for juicing oranges, limes, lemons, grapefruits, and other citrus fruits. You will get the most juice out of these fruits with such a device. These juicers can range in style from a simple handheld reamer, which is good if you're only juicing one fruit, all the way through a countertop press and on to an electric citrus juicer that enables you to juice many fruits in one session. My dad gives us hundreds of lemons from his backyard tree every year. The kids and I take turns juicing them with the electric citrus juicer, to maximize our efficiency. A simple handheld citrus reamer can cost as little as a few bucks, while lower-end electric models start at about $15.

You can juice whole citrus fruits in other types of juicers, which may be quicker and more convenient, particularly when you are juicing several pieces of citrus fruit. But the actual juice yield will be less, and the peel can give the juice a slightly bitter taste, which could be off-putting for some kids. The peel and pith contain phytonutrients not present in the fruit's juicy insides.

CENTRIFUGAL JUICERS

The most common style of juicer, centrifugal juicing machines use a rapidly spinning fine-mesh basket or sieve with a grater on the bottom to shred the fruit or vegetable and separate the fiber from the juice. Some models are "non-ejecting," meaning that they send the juice out a spout but hold the pulp in the juicer until it becomes full. At that point, the machine must be emptied before more juice can be made. An "automatic ejection" model is easier to operate and clean and can produce more juice in one session, since you don't have to stop to clean the machine. As the produce goes into the chute, the pulp is ejected into a canister at the back of the machine while the juice pours out the front spout. Prices for centrifugal juicers start as low as $40 and climb into the $200 range.

Some critics say that centrifugal juicers leave too much juice wasted in the pulp. You can lessen this waste by baking or cooking with the pulp. You can also line the ejection basket with a nut-milk bag or double layer of cheesecloth, then

squeeze it to extract more juice from the fruit or veg. This can be a nice way to get the most from a lower-priced juicer, producing less waste and more juice.

MASTICATING JUICERS

A masticating juicer works more slowly, but is more efficient at extracting juice from the produce. Pieces of fruit are crushed and squeezed by an auger, and the juice is separated from the fiber. More prep work—that is, chopping the fruit—is needed. Since masticating juicers produce less friction and therefore less heat than centrifugal juicers, they are said to retain more of the nutrients in the juice.

These juicers can also produce nut butters, grind coffee and spices, and perform other kitchen tasks. They are more expensive than centrifugal juicers, however. Prices for masticating juicers begin at about $200 but can range as high as $400.

JUICE PRESSES

A juice press is operated by hydraulics that squeeze and press the juice from chopped fruit. Using a juice press is a two-step process in which the fruit is chopped in a food processor or blender and then squeezed in the press to extract the juice. Although there may be a greater yield of juice (and therefore less waste) with this type of juicer than with a centrifugal model, it is more expensive to purchase and less convenient to use. A low-end juice press costs about $300.

BLENDERS

Blenders are ideal smoothie machines. They can crush, grind, and blend fruit, vegetables, and ice quickly and efficiently. Prices range from about $20 for a handheld immersion stick blender to $400 for a heavy-duty model worthy of a smoothie shop. You can also use a food processor to make smoothies, though it might not be as convenient.

Some blenders come with individually sized blender cups, which make cleanup easier and allow you to prepare different variations in quick succession. Alternatively, depending on your blender model, you may be able to screw regular-mouth Mason jars onto your blender base to use as single-serve blender cups.

You can also make juice in a blender or food processor by blending the fruit or vegetables and then straining out the liquid using a nut-milk bag or layered cheesecloth. This isn't the quickest or neatest way to juice, but it can be done. It's an economical shortcut to homemade juice if you don't have the money or counter space for a juicer or if you already own a high-powered blender.

COMPLETE JUICING BLENDERS

There are some blenders that are marketed as "complete juicing machines." Unlike juice extractors, which separate the juice from the pulp, these high-speed blenders liquefy fruit and vegetables—skins, seeds, and all. Juices made with these machines obviously maintain all the fiber of the produce and are, therefore, thicker in consistency than traditional juices. This may take some getting used to, especially for children. The price for this type of blender can range from $100 to several hundred dollars.

Other Fun Equipment

Once you've got the tools to make your juices and smoothies, you might want to consider other kitchen items that help encourage children's enthusiasm about homemade juice. Convenience-food marketers know all too well that kids love bright, novel packaging. Beat them at their own game by making homemade juices fun as well as delicious. Remember that presentation matters, especially with kids.

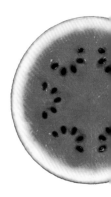

JUICE GLASSES

Back in the day, my grandmother served small glasses of juice at every breakfast. In the 1950s and '60s, decorative juice glasses and colorfully printed jelly jar tumblers were de rigueur. Juice seems more special when it's in a "fancy" glass. Why else would kids fight over what color cup they get? (Clearly, it must improve the flavor!) Search yard sales and thrift stores as well as your favorite kitchen shops for fun juice glasses. They needn't be large, as the ideal serving size is 4 to 6 ounces.

TASTING OR SHOT GLASSES

Two-ounce tasting glasses, or oversized shot glasses, are perfect for little hands. My youngest kids love being served juice in "real glass" glasses. Homemade juice is so flavorful and rich that the smaller serving suits my younger crowd quite well. Plus, the mini portion makes it easy to say "Yes!" to seconds and still stay under a young child's recommended limit for juice.

SMOOTHIE CUPS

Insulated tumblers are ideal for smoothies, especially in the summer months when we want to take our frosty treats outdoors, on the road, and to the pool, where glass is a no-no. Unbreakable cups with lids are ideal for taking juices and smoothies away from home.

For home enjoyment, sturdy half-pint Mason jars make great smoothie vessels, especially when a wide straw is added.

STRAWS

All kids love straws. Let's be honest: Adults do, too! Keep a supply on hand at all times. You can find straws made of paper, plastic, stainless steel, acrylic, and glass. Cocktail straws work well in small glasses.

Straws come in particularly handy when introducing a juice or smoothie that features an unfamiliar flavor and smell. Using a straw and a cup with a lid helps mask any potentially disconcerting aromas, allowing kids to focus on the taste itself.

ICE POP MOLDS

If you're making ice pops from juice, you can use simple, old-school paper cups and food-safe plain wooden craft sticks. But there's a huge selection of plastic ice mold pops available online as well as in retail stores, offering a far greater variety of shapes and sizes. See page 186 for ice pop techniques and hints on what to look for in an ice pop mold.

What Produce Should You Use?

I'm a big believer in shopping the sales. Unless it's a special occasion and I need or want a specific item, I let sales dictate my meal planning—and my juicing as well.

Use what's inexpensive. Buy in-season, organic, and local, whenever possible. I'm not picky about which apples I buy, as long as they are organic and well priced. My target price for fruit is less than $1 per pound. I stock up at that price and try to avoid paying more than that. If you watch the sales and check the different stores in your area, you'll be surprised to find that there are great produce deals to be had. You just need to look for them.

The recipes in this book do not specify particular varieties of fruits or vegetables because availability and prices can vary so much from region to region and from year to year. Feel free to experiment with the recipes, using whichever fruits and vegetables are available and inexpensive. Keep in mind that, in the juices that blend fruit and vegetables, the fruit is often added to offset that veggie flavor that might prompt a child to wrinkle his or her nose. So for those juices, lean on sweeter varieties of apple such as Fuji, Gala, or Braeburn instead of the tarter Granny Smith, for example.

Fruits and vegetables are listed by size (small, medium, and large) rather than weight, with cup measures specified for berries and cubed melon. Juice making is a very flexible process, allowing for some variation of quantities. This is a good thing for us parents. What mom or dad has time to weigh each apple before juicing it while thirsty kids stand at the ready? Don't sweat it if a recipe calls for two large apples and you can only find small ones; just throw in one or two extras and call it good.

Keep in mind that juices will taste best when the fruits are at their peak. A slightly under-ripe plum isn't going to be as flavorful as one that is fully ripe. A watermelon that's imported in winter won't be as tasty as the watermelon your local farmer grows in summer. Using in-season, fully ripe produce will give you the best-tasting juices.

As with all things juicing, remember that your mileage may vary. A given variety of apples or oranges may taste different from shipment to shipment. Grocery stores have different suppliers, so you may get a great bunch of grapes from one shop and a sad, sorry lot from the store down the street. Shop wisely; if you need help, ask the produce manager. They are usually more than happy to assist you in choosing the best produce.

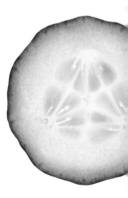

How Do You Prep the Produce?

Different types of juicers require different levels of ingredient prep. Always follow the recommendations made by your juicer's manufacturer. I am generally loath to read instructions, but I read the manual that came with my juicing machine. If I can do it, so can you.

The most basic step is to wash the vegetables and fruit according to their type. Scrub them with a vegetable brush and spray them with a white vinegar rinse made up of three parts water to one part vinegar to kill some germs and remove some pesticides that might be present on the fresh produce. Numerous studies have shown that vinegar is just as effective as commercial produce washes, if not more so. However, similar studies are vague on vinegar's effectiveness against E. coli and salmonella. Take care that your fresh produce does not become cross-contaminated with these harmful bacteria by storing meats separately from fruits and vegetables and by practicing proper kitchen cleanliness.

For masticating juicers, you'll need to chop the fruit and veggies according to the manufacturer's recommendations. If you are using a wide-mouth centrifugal juice extractor, you can use many of your fruits whole. A 3-inch feeding tube allows several carrots to pass through at one time, making for quick juicing. Be sure to follow the manufacturer's recommendations.

I remove any seeds, peel, or pith that I would not normally eat, and I trim any inedible parts, like rotten or bruised spots that might harbor bacteria. These affect the quality of your juice as well as of the pulp that you might use in baking later.

What About the Pulp?

Through the juicing process, the pulp and fiber are separated from the juice. You're obviously going to drink the juice. But what should you do with the pulp that's left over? It seems a shame to waste it.

You don't have to throw out that pulp, which is completely edible. Depending on what type of produce is in the pulp, you can use it in baking and cooking to benefit from the additional fiber and nutrients. Simmer vegetable pulp in savory stocks or mix it into sauces and stews, meat loaves, and meatballs. Stir fruit pulp into pancake batter, muffin mix, or cookie dough. Adapt your favorite carrot cake or zucchini bread to use leftover pulp. See pages 93–95 for recipes that make tasty use of this nutritious pulp.

If you're not planning to bake or cook with the pulp right after juicing, store it in 1- or 2-cup portions in the freezer. Lining the pulp basket with a large zip-top plastic bag makes storage and cleanup particularly easy.

Don't bake? No problem. You can also compost the pulp.

What About Cleaning the Machine?

I'm so glad you asked! Yes, you need to clean up after yourself. Immediately. Do not pass go, do not collect $200, until you've cleaned the machine.

If you're a parent, you know what happens if you leave a child's meal on the table for an hour before cleaning up. The splashes and spills transform into glue that takes extreme elbow grease and more than a little muttering to scrape off. If you had rinsed and wiped right away, you could have saved yourself an hour of frustration.

The same holds true for the juicing machine. Read the manual that comes with your machine to learn exactly how it should be disassembled and cleaned. Commit this to memory and do it as soon as you are done with your juicing session. And be sure to give everything—counters, backsplash, juicing machine base—a good wipe down as well.

How Should You Store Your Juices and Smoothies?

One of the benefits of drinking homemade juices and smoothies is that they are as fresh as it gets. Additives and preservatives are included in the prepackaged versions for a reason: to maintain color and extend the shelf life of the product. To make the most of the nutrients in your homemade drinks, enjoy them the day they're prepared, preferably right away. If you want to pack them for the road or store them in the fridge for a few hours, consider adding a little lemon juice to prevent discoloring. Fresh apple juice in particular turns brown fairly quickly, so drink it up right away.

If you've got leftover juice, don't throw it out. Freeze it! Both juices and smoothies freeze and thaw well. Freeze fresh juices in single-serving cups with lids to make it easy on the other side of thawing. Freezer-safe Mason jars work well for this. You can also make ice pops with leftover juice.

Homemade juices have become a part of our family's food culture. My kids rarely ask for the bottled varieties, because they know how easy it is to make juice at home. They have become adept at identifying flavors that were once foreign. "I think there's a little ginger in this sauce," says a child who might not have known what ginger was a year ago. What was once considered weird has become familiar.

Juices and other homemade drinks are now sought-after treats. Instead of "Can you buy some pop?" I hear "When are you going to make some more of that ginger honey syrup?" Apparently, I've created a new kind of problem. But honestly, I think it's a good problem to have.

Jazzy Fruit Juices

Fruit juices are fun, sweet, and tasty. Consider them a supplement to a healthy diet, not a substitute for regular meals or whole fruit. These juices will be naturally sweeter and more filling than their commercially made counterparts. Add water to taste if you or your children prefer a milder juice.

A Brief History of Juice

Presumably, folks back in the far reaches of time made juice when they had an excess of fruit on hand. It was always consumed fresh, since it would spoil or ferment into alcohol if stored. In 1869, a dentist by the name of Thomas Welch developed a process for pasteurizing grape juice to prevent it from becoming alcoholic. Juices were then bottled or canned using this method. Later, in the 1940s, frozen juice concentrates were developed, with the goal of providing World War II troops with better-tasting juices.

Juicing has long been a great way to use up a glut of fruit that might otherwise spoil or die in a hard freeze. We can take a lesson from history by snatching up fruit when it goes on sale or using excess produce from the garden or orchard. Since we now have the option of freezing, there's no need to worry about pasteurization when preparing your own juice. Drink it fresh or freeze the leftovers.

Pineapple-Pear Juice

Pears and pineapple combine in a rich, frothy drink that is quite filling. Its sunshine yellow hue is sure to be a day brightener.

MAKES 15 TO 20 OUNCES

½ medium pineapple

3 medium pears

1 Trim and core the pineapple. Cut it into spears. Core the pears.

2 Juice the pineapple and pears according to the directions on your juicing machine. Whisk to combine.

3 Add water to taste if you or your children prefer a milder juice.

Apples Galore

In most homes with kids, apple juice is a staple. Making your own apple juice takes the mundane to a new level. You won't want to go back to the bottled variety.

The flavor of your apple juice will vary depending on which variety of apples you use. This blend, made with four sweeter apples and two tart apples, is a lovely taste treat, but feel free to try different varieties. Consider having an apple-and-juice tasting, where kids can try to match the juice to the whole fruit it came from.

MAKES 15 TO 20 OUNCES

2 medium Gala apples

2 medium Fuji apples

2 medium Granny Smith apples

1　Core the apples.

2　Juice the apples according to the directions on your juicing machine. Whisk to combine.

3　Add water to taste if you or your children prefer a milder juice.

Apple-Berry Juice

This juice is one of FishBoy9's absolute favorites. Use whatever berries you have on hand. Add extra apples if berries are in short supply.

MAKES 15 TO 20 OUNCES

> 1½ cups mixed berries (such as strawberries, blueberries, and raspberries)
>
> 2 medium apples

1   Remove the hulls from the strawberries, if using. Core the apples.

2   Juice the berries and apples according to the directions on your juicing machine. Whisk to combine.

3   Add water to taste if you or your children prefer a milder juice.

Apple Pie in a Cup

My children enthusiastically call this "apple pie juice." They recognize the familiar flavors of apple, lemon, and cinnamon from a favorite family dessert. The pears add the sweetness that sugar would provide in a pie.

MAKES 15 TO 20 OUNCES

2 medium pears

2 medium apples

1 Meyer lemon

¼ teaspoon ground cinnamon

1   Core the pears and apples. Peel the lemon, if desired.

2   Juice the pears, apples, and lemon according to the directions on your juicing machine. Whisk to combine.

3   Whisk in the cinnamon.

4   Add water to taste if you or your children prefer a milder juice.

Apples & Oranges

What happens if we put our apples and oranges together? As the old expression has it, these two fruits aren't in any way comparable, but they actually blend quite well together. The vanilla extract gives the juice a sweet, dessert-like surprise.

MAKES 15 TO 20 OUNCES

> 3 medium apples
> 2 medium oranges
> ¼ teaspoon pure vanilla extract

1 Core the apples. Cut the oranges in half.

2 Juice the apples according to the directions on your juicing machine.

3 For a larger yield of juice and less waste, juice the oranges with a citrus juicer or reamer. (If you prefer, you can juice them in the juicing machine, following the manufacturer's directions. Peel the fruit, if desired, prior to juicing.)

4 Whisk the two juices together. Whisk in the vanilla extract.

5 Add water to taste if you or your children prefer a milder juice.

Berry Daze

This berry-based blend is ideal for summer, when these fruits are at their peak. The refreshing, tart flavor of this jewel-colored juice makes it a huge hit. If your berries are *too* tart, add another apple or a pear for a bit of extra sweetness.

MAKES 15 TO 20 OUNCES

    3 cups strawberries
    1 medium apple
    1½ cups blueberries
    1½ cups blackberries

1 Remove the hulls from the strawberries. Core the apple.

2 Juice the berries and apple according to the directions on your juicing machine. Whisk to combine.

3 Add water to taste if you or your children prefer a milder juice.

Golden Tropics

This golden yellow juice is a thick, sweet nectar full of vitamin C. Featuring tropical fruits as well as the familiar orange and grapes, it's a tasty treat.

MAKES 15 TO 20 OUNCES

½ large pineapple

1 small yellow mango (such as Ataulfo)

2 medium kiwis

1 large orange

2 cups seedless green grapes

1 Trim and core the pineapple. Cut it into spears. Peel and pit the mango. Peel the kiwis. Peel the orange, if desired.

2 Juice the pineapple, mango, kiwis, orange, and grapes according to the directions on your juicing machine. Whisk to combine.

3 Add water to taste if you or your children prefer a milder juice.

In the Pink

Most kids I know pick pink or red when choosing Popsicles, punch, or lollipops. This drink will be right up their alley. Strawberries add sweet tartness as well as blushing color to this thick and frothy juice.

MAKES ABOUT 32 OUNCES

3 cups strawberries

½ large pineapple

2 cups seedless green or red grapes

1   Remove the hulls from the strawberries. Trim and core the pineapple. Cut it into spears.

2   Juice the berries, pineapple, and grapes according to the directions on your juicing machine. Whisk to combine.

3   Add water to taste if you or your children prefer a milder juice.

Hot Apple Cider

When sore throats strike or cooler weather arrives, my kids aren't too keen on cold drinks. That's when it's time to make this spiced hot apple cider. Enhanced with orange and lemon juices, it's full of vitamin C to cure whatever ails you.

MAKES 15 TO 20 OUNCES

4 medium apples

1 medium orange

1 small lemon

½ cinnamon stick

6 whole cloves

Honey, to taste (optional)

1 Core the apples. Cut the orange and lemon in half.

2 Juice the apples according to the directions on your juicing machine.

3 For a larger yield of juice and less waste, juice the orange and lemon with a citrus juicer or reamer. (If you prefer, you can juice them in the juicing machine, following the manufacturer's directions. Peel the fruit, if desired, prior to juicing.)

4 Place the two juices, cinnamon stick, and cloves in a small saucepan on the stove. Simmer for 20 minutes over low heat. Add water to taste if you or your children prefer a milder juice.

5 Add honey if you prefer a sweeter juice, and whisk to combine. Serve warm.

Kids' Choice Juice

It makes sense that a kid's favorite fruits will make a kid's favorite juice. Strawberries add vibrant color and a bit of tart flavor to this light pink, frothy juice, while the apples and grapes provide plentiful juice and sweetness.

MAKES 15 TO 20 OUNCES

2 medium apples

1½ cups strawberries

2 cups seedless red or green grapes

1 Core the apples. Remove the hulls from the strawberries.

2 Juice the apples, berries, and grapes according to the directions on your juicing machine. Whisk to combine.

3 Add water to taste if you or your children prefer a milder juice.

Minted Apple-Blueberry Juice

Mint is a fun herb to grow because it's pretty hard to kill. It's also a bit invasive, so be sure to plant it in a pot. It smells great, too. With a backyard mint plant, you can add cooling flavor to any juice, like this combination of blueberries and apples.

MAKES 15 TO 20 OUNCES

3 medium apples

1½ cups blueberries

2 or 3 sprigs fresh mint

1 Core the apples.

2 Juice the apples, blueberries, and mint according to the directions on your juicing machine. Whisk to combine.

3 Add water to taste if you or your children prefer a milder juice.

Tropical Cooler

This greenish-yellow juice is reminiscent of a tropical-fruit-flavored hard candy. It's sweet and tart, with a little kick from the ginger.

MAKES 15 TO 20 OUNCES

2 large kiwis

½ large pineapple

2 cups seedless green grapes

1 (¼- to ½-inch) slice fresh ginger

1 Peel the kiwis. Trim and core the pineapple. Cut it into spears.

2 Juice the kiwis, pineapple, grapes, and ginger according to the directions on your juicing machine. Whisk to combine.

3 Add water to taste if you or your children prefer a milder juice.

Summer in a Cup

Summer berries and watermelon go well with cooling mint. This juice is sweet and refreshing. Surprise and delight your kids with it on the next hot summer day.

MAKES 15 TO 20 OUNCES

> 2 cups strawberries
>
> 2 cups cubed watermelon
>
> 1½ cups blueberries
>
> 2 or 3 sprigs fresh mint

1 Remove the hulls from the strawberries.

2 Juice the strawberries, watermelon, blueberries, and mint according to the directions on your juicing machine. Whisk to combine.

3 Add water to taste if you or your children prefer a milder juice.

Cranberry Fruit Cocktail

Commercially produced cranberry juices are typically laden with added sugar to offset the tart flavor of the cranberries. In this juice, the sweetness comes from other fruits, which also give it its body and bulk.

MAKES 15 TO 20 OUNCES

2 medium pears

1 medium apple

3 cups seedless red grapes

1 cup cranberries

1 Core the pears and apple.

2 Juice the pears, apple, grapes, and cranberries according to the directions on your juicing machine. Whisk to combine.

3 Add water to taste if you or your children prefer a milder juice.

Cranberry-Apple Juice

This tart-sweet juice is always a hit at our house, combining our favorite flavors of fall and winter. Look for sales on cranberries right around the fall holidays. They freeze well, so stock up. Try this with a sweeter variety of apple, like Fuji or Gala, to offset the tartness of the cranberries.

MAKES 15 TO 20 OUNCES

5 medium apples

1 cup cranberries

1 Core the apples.

2 Juice the apples and cranberries according to the directions on your juicing machine. Whisk to combine.

3 Add water to taste if you or your children prefer a milder juice.

Citrus Cooler

This juice is best prepared with a citrus juicer. This—and making sure the fruit is at room temperature—will give you the most juice. Choosing fruit that is particularly heavy for its size also helps maximize yield.

MAKES 15 TO 20 OUNCES

> 5 mandarin oranges
>
> 1 large ruby red grapefruit
>
> 1 large lime

1 Cut each fruit in half.

2 For a larger yield of juice and less waste, juice the fruit with a citrus juicer or reamer. (If you prefer, you can juice them in a juicing machine, following the manufacturer's directions. Peel the fruit, if desired, prior to juicing.) Pour the juice into a pitcher, and whisk to combine.

3 Add water to taste if you or your children prefer a milder juice.

Watermelon-Kiwi Juice

Watermelon and kiwi are fun fruits for kids. Since watermelon is such a juicy fruit, there shouldn't be much pulp left over. If you use a nut-milk bag to line the pulp basket, you can capture and filter every last bit of juice. Save a slice of kiwi to use as an attractive garnish on the glass.

MAKES 15 TO 20 OUNCES

3 large kiwis
2 cups cubed watermelon

1 Peel the kiwis.

2 Juice the kiwis and watermelon according to the directions on your juicing machine. Whisk to combine.

3 Add water to taste if you or your children prefer a milder juice.

Six Ways to Juice on a Budget

It takes a lot of fruit or vegetables to make juice. It may seem like a waste. How can turning all that produce into a few cups of juice be economical? However, homemade juices are clearly less expensive than the store-bought varieties. So, how can we make the most of what we have?

If the recent recession taught us anything, it's that none of us are immune to downturns in the economy. It always helps to be mindful of our spending. Our family has fought the hard battle of unemployment and struggled to get out of debt. I think we're the wiser for it. We've learned how to stretch our resources.

Use these strategies to make homemade juices wisely and economically.

1 **BUY IN SEASON.**

Buy fruits and vegetables in season, choosing locally grown and organic if possible. Not only will they taste better, they are often less expensive, too. Watermelon in winter is bland and pricey. Watermelon in summer is sweet and plentiful.

2 **STOCK UP WHEN YOU SEE A SALE.**

If you juice regularly, you'll be going through vast quantities of certain fruits and vegetables, particularly carrots, apples, and pears. When you see good sales on these items, stock up. Apples and carrots keep for a long time under refrigeration. Buy pears when they are still green and allow them to ripen on the counter. If other fruits or vegetables go on sale during the week, snatch them up and work them into your juices.

3 **FIND IT FOR FREE!**

Keep your eyes and ears open for free produce opportunities. Often folks with backyard gardens and orchards are happy to unload their surplus , as long as you're willing to come to harvest it. Check the want ads for home gardeners giving away their glut of goodies. When you hear friends and family complain of excess produce, by all means offer to take it off their hands.

4 GROW YOUR OWN.

One of the best things my dad ever did was plant a Meyer lemon tree in the backyard. Forty years later, it supplies our families with hundreds of prime citrus fruits every year.

If you've got the space and inclination, plant a fruit tree or garden. With sunshine, water, and a little attention, you can grow your own fruits and vegetables, often for a fraction of the price that the grocery store charges.

5 MAKE FRIENDS WITH YOUR FARMER.

Whether you meet him at the farmers' market or connect with her at the roadside fruit stand, get to know the folks who grow food in your community. Ask how you can get produce at a discount. It may mean picking up what's left over at the end of the market day or swinging by to grab items that are getting too ripe. You might even have the opportunity to trade your time for fruits and vegetables by working the stand for them.

6 JOIN A CSA.

Community-supported agriculture is a great way to connect with and support local farmers. Typically, you subscribe to receive a share of the grower's produce each week, usually paying much less than you would at retail. CSA farmers sometimes offer a "u-pick for free" opportunity for their members. Find out what's available in your community.

Mango Madness

Mangoes are a little tricky to peel and cut, but their flavor makes them well worth the effort. They add a frothy nectar-like consistency to this juice. You'll know a mango is ripe if it gives slightly when pressed gently.

MAKES 15 TO 20 OUNCES

2 small ripe yellow mangoes (such as Ataulfo)

2 medium pears

2 cups seedless red or green grapes

1 Peel and pit the mangoes. Core the pears.

2 Juice the mangoes, pears, and grapes according to the directions on your juicing machine. Whisk to combine.

3 Add water to taste if you or your children prefer a milder juice.

Fish Kids' Fave

Strawberries and watermelon rank as my kids' favorite fruits. I have to fend the bunch of them off in order to make this juice. The resulting concoction is sweet and refreshing, and the kids are always glad I held them at bay.

MAKES 15 TO 20 OUNCES

2 cups strawberries

3 cups cubed watermelon

1 Remove the hulls from the strawberries.

2 Juice the strawberries and watermelon according to the directions on your juicing machine. Whisk to combine.

3 Add water to taste if you or your children prefer a milder juice.

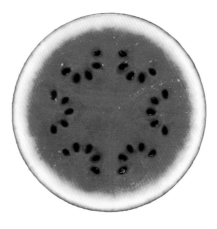

Fruit Salad in a Cup

This mélange of berries, grapes, kiwis, and citrus fruit is full of tart and sweet flavors, reminiscent of a great fruit salad. Its pale pink color makes it a favorite with kids, and its boost of vitamin C makes it a favorite with parents.

MAKES 15 TO 20 OUNCES

1½ cups strawberries

3 large kiwis

1 large ruby red grapefruit

1 medium orange

2 cups seedless red or green grapes

1 Remove the hulls from the strawberries. Peel the kiwis. Cut the grapefruit and orange in half.

2 Juice the strawberries, kiwis, and grapes according to the directions on your juicing machine.

3 For a larger yield of juice and less waste, juice the grapefruit and orange with a citrus juicer or reamer. (If you prefer, you can juice them in the juicing machine, following the manufacturer's directions. Peel the fruit, if desired, prior to juicing.)

4 Pour the two juices into a pitcher, and whisk to combine.

5 Add water to taste if you or your children prefer a milder juice.

The Five-Star Fruit Bowl

What happens when you blend five favorite fruits into a juice? You receive oohs and ahhs from your children, that's what. Mine give this pale pink juice a five-star rating.

MAKES 15 TO 20 OUNCES

1 cup strawberries

1 medium apple

1 medium pear

1 medium orange

2 cups seedless red or green grapes

1 Remove the hulls from the strawberries. Core the apple and pear. Peel the orange, if desired.

2 Juice the strawberries, apple, pear, orange, and grapes according to the directions on your juicing machine. Whisk to combine.

3 Add water to taste if you or your children prefer a milder juice.

Minted Apple-Pear Juice

The pairing of bracing fresh mint and crisp fall fruit works well in this juice. The pears add a luscious creaminess to this frothy juice.

MAKES 15 TO 20 OUNCES

> 2 medium apples
> 2 medium pears
> 3 sprigs fresh mint

1 Core the apples and pears.

2 Juice the apples, pears, and mint according to the directions on your juicing machine. Whisk to combine.

3 Add water to taste if you or your children prefer a milder juice.

Summer Splash

The bounty of summer includes stone fruit and berries. Years ago, when we had a fruit orchard, there was nothing better than walking through it on a cool morning, grabbing breakfast from the trees. Use freestone peaches to make fruit preparation easier.

MAKES 15 TO 20 OUNCES

3 medium peaches or nectarines

3 medium plums

1½ cups blueberries

1 Pit the peaches and plums.

2 Juice the peaches, plums, and blueberries according to the directions on your juicing machine. Whisk to combine.

3 Add water to taste if you or your children prefer a milder juice.

Gingery Orange-Mango Juice

The flavors of ginger, orange, and mango blend well in this kid-pleasing juice. Its vibrant orange color is inviting, making it look like it's full of sunshine.

MAKES 15 TO 20 OUNCES

1 medium red mango
1 medium pear
4 medium oranges
1 (¼- to ½-inch) slice fresh ginger

1   Peel and pit the mango. Core the pear. Cut the oranges in half.

2   Juice the mango, pear, and ginger according to the directions on your juicing machine.

3   For a larger yield of juice and less waste, juice the oranges with a citrus juicer or reamer. (If you prefer, you can juice them in the juicing machine, following the manufacturer's directions. Peel the fruit, if desired, prior to juicing.)

4   Pour the two juices into a pitcher, and whisk to combine.

5   Add water to taste if you or your children prefer a milder juice.

Minty Melons

Summer melons are sweet and bursting with flavor, making them excellent candidates for juicing. The addition of mint lends an extra dimension of refreshing summer flavor.

MAKES 15 TO 20 OUNCES

2 cups cubed honeydew melon

2 cups cubed cantaloupe

2 or 3 sprigs fresh mint

1 Juice the honeydew, cantaloupe, and mint according to the directions on your juicing machine. Whisk to combine.

2 Add water to taste if you or your children prefer a milder juice.

Tropical Peach Juice

Peaches may not be as exotic as their two partners in this juice, but together the three make a great team—especially in summer, when all these fruits are often on sale.

MAKES 15 TO 20 OUNCES

½ large pineapple

2 medium peaches or nectarines

1 large red mango

1 Trim and core the pineapple. Cut it into spears. Pit the peaches. Peel and pit the mango.

2 Juice the pineapple, peaches, and mango according to the directions on your juicing machine. Whisk to combine.

3 Add water to taste if you or your children prefer a milder juice.

Spiced Stone Fruit Juice

Stone fruits are inexpensive and plentiful in summer. They also spoil quickly, so don't let all that seasonal goodness go to waste— use any excess fruit to make juice.

MAKES 15 TO 20 OUNCES

4 medium plums

2 large apricots

2 medium peaches or nectarines (or 1 of each)

2 cups sweet red cherries

¼ teaspoon ground nutmeg

1 Pit the plums, apricots, peaches, and cherries.

2 Juice the plums, apricots, peaches, and cherries according to the directions on your juicing machine. Whisk to combine.

3 Whisk in the nutmeg.

4 Add water to taste if you or your children prefer a milder juice.

Stone Fruit & Grape Juice

Peaches, plums, nectarines, and grapes are all super juicy in the summertime. That's when they offer the best value and the best flavor, too.

MAKES 15 TO 20 OUNCES

2 medium peaches

2 medium nectarines

3 medium plums

2 cups seedless red or green grapes

1   Pit the peaches, nectarines, and plums.

2   Juice the peaches, nectarines, plums, and grapes according to the directions on your juicing machine. Whisk to combine.

3   Add water to taste if you or your children prefer a milder juice.

Life Is Just a Bowl of Cherries

Although cherries might be a little tedious to pit, their flavor makes it well worth the effort, especially when you find the precious summer fruit on sale. Cherry pitters are inexpensive and make the work go much faster. We mix things up here with pear, apricots, and plums for an interesting blend of flavors.

MAKES 15 TO 20 OUNCES

2 cups sweet red cherries

3 medium apricots

3 medium plums

1 large pear

1 Pit the cherries, apricots, and plums. Core the pear.

2 Juice the cherries, apricots, plums, and pear according to the directions on your juicing machine. Whisk to combine.

3 Add water to taste if you or your children prefer a milder juice.

Super Summer Quencher

This particular combination of fruit makes up a favorite summer salad at our house, so it seemed only natural to try them as a juice. Since these fruits are typically extra juicy, line the pulp basket with a nut-milk bag or cheesecloth so that you can extract every bit of juice. There probably will not be much pulp left behind.

MAKES 15 TO 20 OUNCES

2 medium peaches or nectarines

2 medium plums

2 cups cubed watermelon

2 cups seedless red or green grapes

1 Pit the peaches and plums.

2 Juice the peaches, plums, watermelon, and grapes according to the directions on your juicing machine. Whisk to combine.

3 Add water to taste if you or your children prefer a milder juice.

Brilliant Fruit & Vegetable Blends

It's a given that children will gravitate toward sweet fruit juices. Who among us doesn't? But you and your children may be pleasantly surprised to find that fruit-and-vegetable juice blends are equally appealing. They are also a great way to introduce new-to-you vegetable flavors to your family and increase everyone's intake of vitamins and other nutrients.

Mandarin-Apple-Fennel Juice

Fresh fennel adds a slight licorice-anise flavor to this juice, giving it a unique and refreshing twist. The mandarin oranges bring an extra jolt of sweet and tart to this frothy yellow-orange juice.

MAKES 15 TO 20 OUNCES

3 medium apples

½ small fennel bulb with leafy fronds

2 mandarin oranges

1 Core the apples. Quarter the fennel. Cut the oranges in half.

2 Juice the apples and fennel according to the directions on your juicing machine.

3 For a larger yield of juice and less waste, juice the oranges with a citrus juicer or reamer. (If you prefer, you can juice them in the juicing machine, following the manufacturer's directions. Peel the fruit, if desired, prior to juicing.)

4 Pour the two juices into a pitcher, and whisk to combine.

5 Add water to taste if you or your children prefer a milder juice.

Autumn Ade

Carrots and pears are plentiful and inexpensive throughout the fall and winter months, making them perfect partners for leafy fennel. The fennel adds a subtle sweetness and hint of licorice flavor.

MAKES 15 TO 20 OUNCES

3 large carrots

2 medium pears

½ small fennel bulb with leafy fronds

1   Trim the carrots. Core the pears. Quarter the fennel.

2   Juice the carrots, pears, and fennel according to the directions on your juicing machine. Whisk to combine.

3   Add water to taste if you or your children prefer a milder juice.

It's a Keeper

Apples, pears, and carrots are some of the best fresh produce items to keep on hand. Apples and carrots store well and long. Buy pears when they are green, and use them as they ripen on the counter. This pleasing juice is filling and sweet, and it's a standard for the FishKids.

MAKES 15 TO 20 OUNCES

3 large carrots

2 medium apples

1 medium pear

1 Trim the carrots. Core the apples and pear.

2 Juice the carrots, apples, and pear according to the directions on your juicing machine. Whisk to combine.

3 Add water to taste if you or your children prefer a milder juice.

Carrot-Apple Juice

Carrot juice—rich in beta carotene as well as a number of vitamins and minerals—has long been known for its health benefits. However, the flavor can seem a little "earthy" to some people, especially kids. This juice is a nice steppingstone to a pure carrot juice.

MAKES 15 TO 20 OUNCES

3 large carrots

2 medium apples

1   Trim the carrots. Core the apples.

2   Juice the carrots and apples according to the directions on your juicing machine. Whisk to combine.

3   Add water to taste if you or your children prefer a milder juice.

How to Get Your Kids Involved

"Tell me and I forget. Teach me and I remember.
Involve me and I learn."

—BENJAMIN FRANKLIN

My kids have played an integral part in our journey of homemade juices. They've shopped with me, helped prepare fruit and vegetables for juicing, and been keen taste testers in the hunt for the best juices. If you're looking for ways to get your kids involved in your home juicing, consider these tips:

1 SHOW THEM WHERE THEIR FOOD COMES FROM.

Children take an interest in their world and our food supply when they know where the edibles come from. If you can, bring them with you on a trip to a local farm, a stroll through the farmers' market, or a simple run to the grocery store.

Take the time to show them gardening books or cookbooks with illustrations of fruits and vegetables, so that the kids can learn more about the foods they eat. Go berry or apple picking. If you have the space and inclination, plant a fruit tree or a few garden plants in the backyard.

2 LET THE KIDS CHOOSE.

One night I had a brainstorm: take the kids to the store with me and let them choose dessert—from the produce section. The younger three took me up on the offer and were thrilled to do so. When the littles came home with baskets of blueberries and personal-size watermelons, the older kids regretted their decision to stay home. Luckily for them, they've got generous siblings.

My kids were absolutely giddy over their choice of fruits, possibly more so than if I had taken them to the ice cream shop.

I've learned that it's valuable to let kids help choose the fruits and vegetables we juice, too. They are more likely to try the juice and more likely to love it. Having ownership over the experience increases their interest in it.

3 LISTEN TO THEIR FEEDBACK.

All people appreciate it when you respect their opinions and wishes. Kids are no different. When we value their feedback, we show that we respect them. My kids don't love the flavor of celery juice. I keep this in mind and limit its use. Likewise, if there's a certain juice they prefer, I try to make that one often.

4 LET THEM DO IT.

Teach your children kitchen skills—it will serve them well for life. Prepping fruits and vegetables for juicing is an easy activity for kids. The littlest ones can wash and scrub the produce, while older kids can help trim carrot tops or peel oranges. My friend Stacy preps the vegetables for juicing, but her son does the actual juicing.

Include your kids in meal prep whenever possible. This teaches them valuable life skills and increases their interest in culinary endeavors.

5 MAKE JUICE, NOT WAR.

Remember that it's a process. Not every kid will like every juice or smoothie. Not every kid will like participating in the kitchen—at first. But if you make kitchen prep a regular activity, your kids will learn to see it as normative. Keep it positive.

Eventually, your kids will come to have a sense of ownership over their own food choices. They'll know the right choices to make because you taught them. And chances are, if their experiences have been positive ones, they'll continue to make good food choices long after you stop buying their groceries.

And that's really the point of all this, isn't it?

The Produce Basket

This bright pink juice, one of our favorites, includes a large variety of common fruits and vegetables.

MAKES 20 TO 25 OUNCES

2 medium pears
1 medium apple
1 large carrot
1 medium beet
2 medium oranges
1 medium lemon
1 medium lime

1 Core the pears and apple. Trim the carrot. Trim, peel, and quarter the beet. Cut the oranges, lemon, and lime in half.

2 Juice the pears, apple, carrot, and beet according to the directions on your juicing machine.

3 For a larger yield of juice, juice the oranges, lemon, and lime with a citrus juicer or reamer. (If you prefer, you can juice them in the juicing machine, following the manufacturer's directions. Peel the fruit, if desired, prior to juicing.)

4 Pour the two juices into a pitcher, and whisk to combine.

5 Add water to taste if you or your children prefer a milder juice.

Summer Harvest

Zucchini is both prolific and easily hidden in sweeter fare such as zucchini bread and chocolate-zucchini cake. Here, it makes an appearance with sweet summer fruit.

MAKES 15 TO 20 OUNCES

3 medium peaches

1 large carrot

1 medium zucchini

1 cup blueberries

1 Pit the peaches. Trim the carrot and zucchini.

2 Juice the peaches, carrot, zucchini, and blueberries according to the directions on your juicing machine. Whisk to combine.

3 Add water to taste if you or your children prefer a milder juice.

Oh My Darling Clementine

This juice gets its name and its distinct orange flavor from just one clementine. Juicing this type of mandarin orange whole, with its peel and pith, adds an extra punch of flavor as well as nutrients. The ginger contributes a warm zip, but feel free to use a smaller slice of ginger, if you prefer.

MAKES 15 TO 20 OUNCES

3 large carrots

2 medium pears

2 medium apples

1 clementine

1 (½- to 1-inch) slice fresh ginger

1 Trim the carrots. Core the pears and apples.

2 Juice the carrots, pears, apples, clementine, and ginger according to the directions on your juicing machine. Whisk to combine.

3 Add water to taste if you or your children prefer a milder juice.

Zip-a-Dee-Doo-Dah

The lime and ginger add great flavor and zip to this juice: The lime brings sweetness to the table, while the ginger warms things up. This juice, with its easy-to-keep-on-hand ingredients, is one of our favorites.

MAKES 15 TO 20 OUNCES

> 3 medium Granny Smith apples
> 3 large carrots
> 1 medium lime
> 1 (½- to 1-inch) slice fresh ginger

1 Core the apples. Trim the carrots. Peel the lime, if desired.

2 Juice the apples, carrots, lime, and ginger according to the directions on your juicing machine. Whisk to combine.

3 Add water to taste if you or your children prefer a milder juice.

Tickled Pink

The beet lends a pink color to this juice that my younger daughter just can't resist. The different colors layer atop one another in the juice pitcher, making a beautiful rainbow of flavor. Admire it with your kids before going at it with the whisk.

MAKES 15 TO 20 OUNCES

6 large carrots
3 medium pears
1 medium beet

1. Trim the carrots. Core the pears. Trim, peel, and quarter the beet.

2. Juice the carrots, pears, and beet according to the directions on your juicing machine. Whisk to combine.

3. Add water to taste if you or your children prefer a milder juice.

Fruits & Veggies

The scent of kale may put off some kids, but the juice is quite sweet, thanks to the apples. Using a lidded cup and a straw hides the aroma, making it easier to enjoy the sweet mixture.

MAKES 15 TO 20 OUNCES

2 medium apples

2 large carrots

1 medium beet

1 medium pear

1 medium orange

1 medium lime

4 leaves kale

2 stalks fennel with leafy fronds (not the bulb)

1 Core the apples. Trim the carrots. Trim, peel, and quarter the beet. Core the pear. Cut the orange and lime in half.

2 Juice the apples, carrots, beet, pear, kale, and fennel according to the directions on your juicing machine.

3 For a larger yield of juice and less waste, juice the orange and lime with a citrus juicer or reamer. (If you prefer, you can juice them in the juicing machine, following the manufacturer's directions. Peel the fruit, if desired, prior to juicing.)

4 Pour the two juices into a pitcher, and whisk to combine.

5 Add water to taste if you or your children prefer a milder juice.

Winter Avalanche

This sweet and flavorful juice showcases winter fruits, and the ginger adds a nice punch. It has lots of essential vitamin C to help combat those winter colds. Leaving the orange unpeeled will add the extra nutrients found in the pith and peel, but if you prefer, you can peel the orange.

MAKES 15 TO 20 OUNCES

2 large carrots

2 large apples

1 medium pear

1 mandarin orange

1 (¼-inch) slice fresh ginger

1 Trim the carrots. Core the apples and pear.

2 Juice the carrots, apples, pear, orange, and ginger according to the directions on your juicing machine. Whisk to combine.

3 Add water to taste if you or your children prefer a milder juice.

Orange You Glad?

Serve this juice up with a generous helping of knock-knock jokes to complement its vivid orange color. Juicing the oranges in a citrus juicer will yield the most juice. Even kids who disdain sweet potatoes won't realize that one is in here.

MAKES 15 TO 20 OUNCES

2 large carrots

1 large orange sweet potato or garnet yam

2 medium oranges

1 (½-inch) slice fresh ginger

1   Trim the carrots. Peel the sweet potato. Cut the oranges in half.

2   Juice the carrots, sweet potato, and ginger according to the directions on your juicing machine.

3   For a larger yield of juice and less waste, juice the oranges with a citrus juicer or reamer. (If you prefer, you can juice them in the juicing machine, following the manufacturer's directions. Peel the fruit, if desired, prior to juicing.)

4   Pour the two juices into a pitcher, and whisk to combine.

5   Add water to taste if you or your children prefer a milder juice.

I Yam What I Yam

My kids aren't huge fans of sweet potatoes, but I know that the orange tuber is rich in vitamins and beta carotene. Juicing them has been a good way to get my kids more accustomed to the flavor without the texture they dislike getting in the way.

MAKES 15 TO 20 OUNCES

> 3 large carrots
>
> 2 medium orange sweet potatoes or garnet yams
>
> 1 medium navel orange
>
> 1 medium lime
>
> 1 (¼- to ½-inch) slice fresh ginger

1 Trim the carrots. Peel the sweet potatoes. Cut the orange and lime in half.

2 Juice the carrots, sweet potatoes, and ginger according to the directions on your juicing machine.

3 For a larger yield of juice and less waste, juice the orange and lime with a citrus juicer or reamer. (If you prefer, you can juice them in the juicing machine, following the manufacturer's directions. Peel the fruit, if desired, prior to juicing.)

4 Pour the two juices into a pitcher, and whisk to combine.

5 Add water to taste if you or your children prefer a milder juice.

Spiced Carrot-Orange Juice

The combination of carrots, oranges, ginger, and cinnamon is both sweet and refreshing. The addition of a pear lends a creamy texture to the juice. FishBoy11 describes this as "so delicious and exotic." The kid's ready for Food Network, I'm sure.

MAKES 15 TO 20 OUNCES

3 medium carrots

1 medium pear

3 medium oranges

1 (¼-inch) slice fresh ginger

¼ teaspoon ground cinnamon

1 Trim the carrots. Core the pear. Cut the oranges in half.

2 Juice the carrots, pear, and ginger according to the directions on your juicing machine.

3 For a larger yield of juice and less waste, juice the oranges with a citrus juicer or reamer. (If you prefer, you can juice them in the juicing machine, following the manufacturer's directions. Peel the fruit, if desired, prior to juicing.)

4 Pour the two juices into a pitcher, and whisk to combine. Whisk in the cinnamon.

5 Add water to taste if you or your children prefer a milder juice.

Apples, Oranges, & . . . Broccoli

Yes, broccoli in a juice! This concoction boasts a pretty green color and a super-sweet taste. Savvy sniffers might detect the scent of broccoli, but the taste is mild. If you typically serve only the florets of the broccoli, save the stalks for this recipe.

MAKES 15 TO 20 OUNCES

3 medium apples

1 small head broccoli

3 broccoli stalks or another small head broccoli

1 clementine

1 (¼- to ½-inch) slice fresh ginger

1   Core the apples. Trim and cut the broccoli head and stalks. Peel the clementine, if desired.

2   Juice the apples, broccoli, clementine, and ginger according to the directions on your juicing machine. Whisk to combine.

3   Add water to taste if you or your children prefer a milder juice.

Minted Fall Fruits & Veg

This bright orange juice, with a hint of apple goodness and bright mint undertones, gets its sweetness from pears and carrots. It's just a happy, happy juice.

MAKES 15 TO 20 OUNCES

3 medium apples

2 medium pears

3 medium carrots

3 sprigs fresh mint

1 Core the apples and pears. Trim the carrots.

2 Juice the apples, pears, carrots, and mint according to the directions on your juicing machine. Whisk to combine.

3. Add water to taste if you or your children prefer a milder juice.

I Feel Good!

My kids love a particular powdered vitamin C supplement that you add to water. This juice tastes just like it and is a natural source of vitamins and antioxidants, perfect for making you feel good.

MAKES 15 TO 20 OUNCES

4 medium carrots
4 medium apples
1 medium orange
1 (¼- to ½-inch) slice fresh ginger

1 Trim the carrots. Core the apples. Peel the orange, if desired.

2 Juice the carrots, apples, orange, and ginger according to the directions on your juicing machine. Whisk to combine.

3 Add water to taste if you or your children prefer a milder juice.

Waste Not, Want Not

One of my goals as a mom and family manager is to be a good steward of our resources. A grandchild of folks who survived the Great Depression, I haven't forgotten the value of a dime—or a good peach.

I regularly save the fruit and vegetable pulp left from a juicing session to use in baking. I line the pulp canister with a plastic bag for ease of cleaning. If I'm not ready to bake just then, I use a zip-top plastic storage bag to stash the pulp in the freezer for use at a later date. I label the bag so I know what flavors I'll be incorporating into my baked goods. Waste not, want not. In this way, I always have something to stir into baked goods to add both flavor and fiber.

Most of us have favorite go-to recipes for carrot cake, zucchini bread, and berry muffins. Consider substituting pulp for the fruit in your recipe. If it's a recipe you know well, you'll be able to estimate if it needs a tablespoon or more of liquid to compensate for the moisture missing from very dry pulp.

The following recipes work well with all apple, pear, and carrot pulps, as well as some of the greens. Very juicy fruits like melons won't really produce much pulp, so avoid using those. I've used kale or spinach pulp mixed with other fruits in chocolate cake, and the greens are barely noticeable. Before mixing up a batter, be sure to remove any chunks of carrot or apple peel that might have sneaked into the pulp basket during juicing. Baking with pulp is a little bit of an experiment, the variables being your juicing machine, your recipe, and the fruit or vegetable pulp you have on hand. Approach it with an open mind.

Sunshine Snack Muffins

These maple-sweetened spice muffins get fiber and nutrients from the pulp. They make a tasty breakfast or snack-time treat. Feel free to use unbleached all-purpose flour if you can't find white whole wheat. Freeze cooled, baked muffins in freezer bags to enjoy at a later date, if you like.

MAKES 12 MUFFINS

1½ cups white whole-wheat flour

1½ teaspoons baking soda

1 teaspoon ground cinnamon

½ teaspoon ground nutmeg

½ teaspoon ground ginger

½ teaspoon salt

½ cup plain yogurt

½ cup sunflower oil

½ cup pure maple syrup

2 large eggs

¼ cup milk

1 teaspoon vanilla extract

1 cup fruit-and-vegetable pulp, left over from juicing

½ cup sliced almonds, plus additional for sprinkling

½ cup dark or golden raisins

1 Preheat the oven to 350°F. Line a 12-cup muffin pan with paper liners.

2 In a large bowl, whisk together the flour, baking soda, cinnamon, nutmeg, ginger, and salt.

3 In a separate large bowl, whisk together the yogurt, oil, maple syrup, eggs, and milk. Stir in the vanilla extract and the pulp.

4 Gently add the wet ingredients to the dry, folding to combine. Fold in the ½ cup almonds and the raisins.

5 Divide the batter among the muffin cups. Sprinkle the tops with the additional sliced almonds.

6 Bake for 20 minutes or until a tester inserted in the center of a muffin comes out clean.

7 Cool the muffins on a wire rack before serving.

Chocolate Bundt Cake

This chocolate bundt cake is great for snacking. An adaptation of my recipe for chocolate-zucchini cake, it's less sweet than most cakes, but it offers enough flavor to satisfy a craving.

SERVES 16

2⅓ cups unbleached all-purpose flour

⅓ cup natural unsweetened cocoa powder

2 teaspoons baking powder

2 teaspoons baking soda

2 teaspoons ground cinnamon

1 teaspoon salt

1 cup honey

¾ cup sunflower oil

3 large eggs

2 teaspoons vanilla extract

2 cups fruit-and-vegetable pulp, left over from juicing

½ cup milk

1. Preheat the oven to 350°F. Spray a bundt pan with nonstick cooking spray.

2. In a large bowl, sift together the flour, cocoa, baking powder, baking soda, cinnamon, and salt.

3. In a separate large bowl, whisk together the honey and oil until smooth. Add the eggs, one at a time, beating well after each addition. Stir in the vanilla extract and the pulp.

4. Alternately stir the dry ingredients and the milk into the wet ingredients.

5. Pour the batter into the prepared pan. Bake for 45 minutes, or until a tester inserted in the center comes out with just a few crumbs attached.

6. Cool the cake in the pan on a wire rack for 15 minutes. Carefully run a rubber spatula around the edges of the pan to loosen the cake. Invert the cake onto a cooling rack and remove the pan. Cool the cake completely before serving.

Surprise Pudding Cake

My kids always ask, "What's in this?" I answer, "It's a surprise." And of course, it is. They're skeptical at first, but the cake is always devoured within the hour. Use naturally sweetened chocolate chips if you can; otherwise, splurge on the conventional type, which do contain sugar. (But hey, it's only half a cup of chips!)

SERVES 8

½ cup unbleached all-purpose flour

½ cup natural unsweetened cocoa powder

½ teaspoon baking powder

½ teaspoon salt

½ cup honey

½ cup sunflower oil

2 large eggs

1 teaspoon pure vanilla extract

1½ cups fruit-and-vegetable pulp, left over from juicing

½ cup chocolate chips

1 Preheat the oven to 350°F. Spray an 8-inch square baking pan with nonstick cooking spray.

2 In a large bowl, whisk together the flour, cocoa, baking powder, and salt.

3 In a separate large bowl, whisk together the honey and oil until smooth. Add the eggs, one at a time, beating well after each addition. Stir in the vanilla extract and the pulp.

4 Fold the dry mixture into the wet ingredients. Fold in the chocolate chips.

5 Pour the batter into the prepared pan. Bake for 20 to 25 minutes, or until a tester inserted in the center comes out with just a few crumbs attached.

6 Cool on a wire rack before serving.

Super Green

Don't judge a juice by its color. When my son saw this one, he said, "It looks like your guacamole." But looks, as we know, can be deceiving. This avocado-green juice is a sweet and fruity delight.

MAKES 15 TO 20 OUNCES

2 medium pears

2 medium apples

2 leaves Swiss chard

1 Core the pears and apples.

2 Juice the pears, apples, and chard according to the directions on your juicing machine. Whisk to combine.

3 Add water to taste if you or your children prefer a milder juice.

Gingery Apple–Carrot Juice

This simple juice is both refreshing and comforting. The ginger provides a bit of spicy zip, while the apples and carrots add sweetness and flavor. It's a big favorite at our house.

MAKES 15 TO 20 OUNCES

4 medium carrots

3 medium apples

1 (¼- to ½-inch) slice fresh ginger

1 Trim the carrots. Core the apples.

2 Juice the carrots, apples, and ginger according to the directions on your juicing machine. Whisk to combine.

3 Add water to taste if you or your children prefer a milder juice.

Strawberry Fields

This sweet, bright orange juice makes me feel joyful and relaxed. My young testers say it "tastes like summer." The addition of early strawberries to long-storing carrots and apples lets you know that summer really is coming soon.

MAKES 15 TO 20 OUNCES

3 medium carrots

2 medium apples

1½ cups strawberries

1 Trim the carrots. Core the apples. Remove the hulls from the strawberries.

2 Juice the carrots, apples, and strawberries according to the directions on your juicing machine. Whisk to combine.

3 Add water to taste if you or your children prefer a milder juice.

Sweet Tarts

While some folks aren't fans of beets, that's not been the case at our house. My younger daughter loves the pink color the beets provide, and the rest of us appreciate their sweetness. This juice is fabulous: sweet from the blend of fruits and vegetables, yet a bit tart from the lime.

MAKES 15 TO 20 OUNCES

3 medium apples

3 large carrots

1 medium beet

1 medium lime

1   Core the apples. Trim the carrots. Trim, peel, and quarter the beet. Peel the lime, if desired.

2   Juice the apples, carrots, beet, and lime according to the directions on your juicing machine. Whisk to combine.

3   Add water to taste if you or your children prefer a milder juice.

Ruby Red Pick-Me-Up

This vibrant red drink shines with a sweet-tart flavor that pleases both kids and adults. FishPapa agrees. The oranges add tartness, while the parsnips and carrots contribute a woodsy note. The beet, apple, and pear mellow and sweeten the juice.

MAKES 20 TO 25 OUNCES

5 leaves kale

3 medium oranges

2 large carrots

2 medium parsnips

1 large beet

1 medium apple

1 medium pear

1 Remove any thick, woody stems from the kale. Cut the oranges in half. Trim the carrots. Trim the parsnips. Peel and quarter the beet. Core the apple and pear.

2 Juice the kale, carrots, parsnips, beet, apple, and pear according to the directions on your juicing machine.

3 For a larger yield of juice and less waste, juice the oranges with a citrus juicer or reamer. (If you prefer, you can juice them in the juicing machine, following the manufacturer's directions. Peel the fruit, if desired, prior to juicing.)

What's in Season?

Knowing which fruits and vegetables are in season will help you buy the right produce at the right time. Some fruits and vegetables, such as bananas, are readily available and delicious all year round, but most still have a special "peak" season. Consult these lists for the 411 on what's in season and when to look for specials. Keep in mind that availability may depend on where you live and the growing conditions in a particular year.

SPRING

Apricots
Avocados
Radishes
Strawberries
Sweet cherries

SUMMER

Avocados
Basil
Bell peppers
Blueberries
Boysenberries
Cantaloupe
Cucumbers
Honeydew
Mangoes
Mint
Peaches

Plums
Raspberries
Tomatoes
Watermelon
Zucchini and summer squash

FALL

Apples
Figs
Grapes
Kale
Pears
Pomegranates
Pumpkin
Winter squash
Spinach
Sweet potatoes
Swiss chard

WINTER

Beets
Broccoli
Cabbage
Carrots
Celery
Clementines
Cranberries
Fennel
Grapefruit
Kiwis
Lemons
Limes
Mandarin oranges
Oranges
Parsnips
Tangerines

4 Pour the two juices into a pitcher, and whisk to combine.

5 Add water to taste if you or your children prefer a milder juice.

Can't Beet This

Even the pickiest eaters might be persuaded to enjoy broccoli when it's juiced along with sweet apples and beets. This bright magenta concoction is quite pretty, too.

MAKES 15 TO 20 OUNCES

3 medium apples

1 small head broccoli

1 large beet

1 Core the apples. Trim and cut up the broccoli head and stalks. Trim, peel, and quarter the beet.

2 Juice the apples, broccoli, and beet according to the directions on your juicing machine. Whisk to combine.

3 Add water to taste if you or your children prefer a milder juice.

Berry-Carrot Juice

This is another five-star juice, according to the FishKids.
"Mmm . . . I love this," they say, one after another.

MAKES 15 TO 20 OUNCES

4 large carrots

2 cups strawberries

1 Trim the carrots. Remove the hulls from the strawberries.

2 Juice the carrots and strawberries according to the directions on your juicing machine. Whisk to combine.

3 Add water to taste if you or your children prefer a milder juice.

Autumn Harvest

This sweet, coral-colored juice combines hearty carrots, creamy pears, and tart cranberries. Fall is the perfect time to enjoy this juice, when all the ingredients are in season and well priced.

MAKES 15 TO 20 OUNCES

5 medium carrots

2 medium pears

1 cup cranberries

1 Trim the carrots. Core the pears.

2 Juice the carrots, pears, and cranberries according to the directions on your juicing machine. Whisk to combine.

3 Add water to taste if you or your children prefer a milder juice.

Orange Wow

Butternut squash is highly nutritious, but it causes some kids to balk. They won't know what wowed them when they taste this juice. Telling them is up to you.

MAKES 15 TO 20 OUNCES

> 1 medium butternut squash
> 1 large red mango
> 1 large orange
> 1 (¼- to ½-inch) slice fresh ginger

1 Peel and seed the squash. Cut it into large chunks. Peel and pit the mango. Peel the orange, if desired.

2 Juice the squash, mango, orange, and ginger according to the directions on your juicing machine. Whisk to combine.

3 Add water to taste if you or your children prefer a milder juice.

Peachy Keen

This peachy juice gets its sweetness from a couple of sources: apricots and peaches. Carrots and kale add an earthy note, while the ginger contributes powerful flavor and plenty of antioxidants.

MAKES 15 TO 20 OUNCES

3 medium carrots

3 medium peaches

3 large apricots

2 large kale leaves

1 (¼- to ½-inch) slice fresh ginger

1   Trim the carrots. Pit the peaches and apricots.

2   Juice the carrots, peaches, apricots, kale, and ginger according to the directions on your juicing machine. Whisk to combine.

3   Add water to taste if you or your children prefer a milder juice.

This & That

This juice has a little of this from the veggie drawer and a little of that from the fruit bowl. Don't let its, shall we say, earthy color deceive you. At my house, the resulting mixture is greeted with "Delicious!" and "More, please"—music to a mother's ears.

MAKES 15 TO 20 OUNCES

3 medium carrots

2 medium apples

2 mandarin oranges

1 handful spinach leaves

1 (3-inch) chunk cucumber

1 (¼- to ½-inch) slice fresh ginger

1 Trim the carrots. Core the apples. Cut the mandarin oranges in half.

2 Juice the carrots, apples, spinach, cucumber, and ginger according to the directions on your juicing machine.

3 For a larger yield of juice and less waste, juice the oranges with a citrus juicer or reamer. (If you prefer, you can juice them in the juicing machine, following the manufacturer's directions. Peel the fruit, if desired, prior to juicing.)

4 Pour the two juices into a pitcher, and whisk to combine.

5 Add water to taste if you or your children prefer a milder juice.

Vivacious Veggie-Centric Juices

Vegetable-only juices can sound ominous to some kids.
They might shy away from cooked or raw veggies—or both!—so
the idea of putting these ingredients in a juice may prompt a child
to raise an eyebrow or wrinkle a nose. It doesn't mean they aren't
good for them or even tasty. Savvy kids will admit that as well.

To ease the transition for children, I've incorporated a token
fruit into many of these veggie-centric juices. Sweeter items
like apples and oranges can add a hint of familiarity that makes
these juices more kid friendly. I've found that over time, with
repetition, my kids often come to enjoy flavors that were once
foreign to them. Every child is unique, but keep trying!

Carrot-Apple-Celery Juice

This vegetable-and-apple combo, with its sweet-tartness, is reminiscent of lemonade. The celery here adds an interesting savory flavor that may be a little surprising (in a good way).

MAKES 15 TO 20 OUNCES

3 large carrots
2 medium apples
1 rib celery

1 Trim the carrots. Core the apples. Trim the celery.

2 Juice the carrots, apples, and celery according to the directions on your juicing machine. Whisk to combine.

3 Add water to taste if you or your children prefer a milder juice.

Vegging Out

This juice passes muster with even my most finicky child. He concedes that the vegetable flavor is strong, but he doesn't object to it. The pears do a nice job of sweetening things up.

MAKES 15 TO 20 OUNCES

> 3 large carrots
>
> 2 medium pears
>
> ½ medium fennel bulb, trimmed
>
> 4 kale leaves

1 Trim the carrots. Core the pears. Quarter the fennel.

2 Juice the carrots, pears, fennel, and kale according to the directions on your juicing machine. Whisk to combine.

3 Add water to taste if you or your children prefer a milder juice.

Gazpacho Juice

This juice tastes like salsa in a glass—but without the spice. Feel free to add a few dashes of hot pepper sauce for those who like a little kick. You will find yourself craving tortilla chips to munch alongside this drink.

MAKES 15 TO 20 OUNCES

2 medium tomatoes

1 medium cucumber

1 large red bell pepper

1 medium lime

½ small red onion

2 handfuls fresh cilantro

1 Core the tomatoes. Trim the cucumber. Core and seed the pepper. Peel the lime, if desired.

2 Juice the tomatoes, cucumber, bell pepper, lime, onion, and cilantro according to the directions on your juicing machine. Whisk to combine.

3 Add water to taste if you or your children prefer a milder juice.

Uncharded Territory

This juice, which is mostly made from vegetables, has been deemed "very good" by FishBoy9, a.k.a. Mr. Picky. What a surprise from the kid who "doesn't like vegetables very much." Clearly, we've entered uncharted territory.

MAKES 15 TO 20 OUNCES

3 medium carrots

2 medium parsnips

2 medium pears

2 small beets

3 leaves Swiss chard

1 Trim the carrots and parsnips. Core the pears. Trim, peel, and quarter the beets.

2 Juice the carrots, parsnips, pears, beets, and chard according to the directions on your juicing machine. Whisk to combine.

3 Add water to taste if you or your children prefer a milder juice.

Carrots & Broccoli

Here's a great way to get kids to drink their broccoli! The broccoli flavor is noticeable at the first sip of this earth-toned juice, but it mellows as you go along. The orange adds sweetness.

MAKES 15 TO 20 OUNCES

5 medium carrots

1 small head broccoli

1 large parsnip

1 medium orange

1 small beet

1 Trim the carrots, broccoli, and parsnip. Peel the orange, if desired. Trim, peel, and quarter the beet.

2 Juice the carrots, broccoli, parsnip, orange, and beet according to the directions on your juicing machine. Whisk to combine.

3 Add water to taste if you or your children prefer a milder juice.

Winter Rainbow

This simple juice makes use of the produce mainstays of winter. The carrots and apples add sweetness. You can use kale or spinach instead of chard, if you like.

MAKES 15 TO 20 OUNCES

3 medium carrots

2 medium apples

6 or 7 leaves rainbow Swiss chard

1 Trim the carrots. Core the apples.

2 Juice the carrots, apples, and chard according to the directions on your juicing machine. Whisk to combine.

3 Add water to taste if you or your children prefer a milder juice.

We Got the Beet!

I realize I'm showing my age, but whenever I cut up beets, I can't help but sing "We got the beet, yeah!" This bright pink juice is sweet yet hearty.

MAKES 15 TO 20 OUNCES

> 5 medium carrots
>
> 2 medium pears
>
> 1 large beet

1 Trim the carrots. Core the pears. Trim, peel, and quarter the beet.

2 Juice the carrots, pears, and beet according to the directions on your juicing machine. Whisk to combine.

3 Add water to taste if you or your children prefer a milder juice.

On the Greener Side

This veggie-centric juice is heavy on the vegetables and full of nutrients. Feel free to trade out the chard for spinach or kale, if that's what you have on hand. The celery can be a bit much for some kids. If those kids happen to be yours, you can omit the celery or reduce it by half.

MAKES 15 TO 20 OUNCES

3 medium carrots
2 medium parsnips
1 rib celery
1 medium pear
8 leaves Swiss chard

1 Trim the carrots, parsnips, and celery. Core the pear.

2 Juice the carrots, parsnips, celery, pear, and chard according to the directions on your juicing machine. Whisk to combine.

3 Add water to taste if you or your children prefer a milder juice.

A Little Parsnippety

Before our family started making juices, we didn't really care for parsnips. However, we've found them to be a welcome addition to juice. Now, when we get a supply in the produce box, we don't have to pawn them off on the neighbors. We make juice instead.

MAKES 15 TO 20 OUNCES

4 medium carrots

2 medium parsnips

1 rib celery

1 medium apple

1 (¼- to ½-inch) slice fresh ginger

1 Trim the carrots, parsnips, and celery. Core the apple.

2 Juice the carrots, parsnips, celery, apple, and ginger according to the directions on your juicing machine. Whisk to combine.

3 Add water to taste if you or your children prefer a milder juice.

The Iron Man

Fans of Tony Stark will be familiar with his healthy green juice. This juice is a rich red-gold, more like the Iron Man suit, thanks to the red chard. For a greener juice, use green chard instead. Either way, it's full of good stuff, to help make you strong enough to fight the bad guys.

MAKES 15 TO 20 OUNCES

2 medium apples

2 medium carrots

1 rib celery

4 leaves red Swiss chard

2 handfuls spinach

2 handfuls curly endive

1 (¼- to ½-inch) slice fresh ginger

1 Core the apples. Trim the carrots and celery.

2 Juice the apples, carrots, celery, chard, spinach, endive, and ginger according to the directions on your juicing machine. Whisk to combine.

3 Add water to taste if you or your children prefer a milder juice.

Hearty-Har-Harvest

This hearty juice flavored with a touch of mint is full of vegetables that kids might ignore when presented on a plate. But a glass of this red-orange juice goes down with ease.

MAKES 15 TO 20 OUNCES

2 medium apples

2 medium carrots

1 medium orange sweet potato or garnet yam

6 leaves red Swiss chard

2 handfuls curly endive

2 or 3 sprigs fresh mint

1 Core the apples. Trim the carrots. Peel the sweet potato.

2 Juice the apples, carrots, sweet potato, chard, endive, and mint according to the directions on your juicing machine. Whisk to combine.

3 Add water to taste if you or your children prefer a milder juice.

Red Hots

This juice, though full of vegetables, tastes rather remarkably like the spicy candy Red Hots, thanks to the cinnamon and the sweetness of the apples and beets.

MAKES 15 TO 20 OUNCES

3 medium carrots

2 medium beets

2 medium apples

5 leaves kale

½ teaspoon ground cinnamon

1 Trim the carrots. Trim, peel, and quarter the beets. Core the apples.

2 Juice the carrots, beets, apples, and kale according to the directions on your juicing machine. Whisk to combine.

3 Whisk in the cinnamon.

4 Add water to taste if you or your children prefer a milder juice.

Veg Eight

This all-vegetable juice is a nod to the traditional blend you might have known as a child. It gets its sweetness and ruby red color from the beet and tomato. For some kids, its very veggie-ness may take some getting used to, so consider it an "intermediate level" juice.

MAKES 15 TO 20 OUNCES

1 medium carrot

1 rib celery

1 large beet

1 medium tomato

1 medium red bell pepper

2 leaves red Swiss chard

1 handful spinach leaves

1 (3-inch) chunk cucumber

1 Trim the carrot and celery. Trim, peel, and quarter the beet. Core the tomato. Core and seed the pepper.

2 Juice the carrot, celery, beet, tomato, pepper, chard, spinach, and cucumber according to the directions on your juicing machine. Whisk to combine.

3 Add water to taste if you or your children prefer a milder juice.

The Dirty Dozen and the Clean Fifteen

It's common knowledge that organic produce, grown without chemical fertilizers and pesticides, is better for the environment and better for our health. In an ideal world, we'd be buying all organic.

Unfortunately, organic produce still costs more at the checkout than conventionally grown produce. Until that changes, we sometimes find ourselves in a quandary about what to buy. If you have to choose between best quality and better pricing, the Dirty Dozen list can at least help you know what to avoid.

Each year the Environmental Working Group, a research and advocacy organization, releases lists of the Dirty Dozen and the Clean Fifteen. These lists identify the fruits and vegetables that have the highest and lowest levels, respectively, of pesticide residue from conventional farming. It might be worth spending the extra money for organic versions of items on the Dirty Dozen list. But you can save a few pennies by buying conventionally grown produce from the Clean Fifteen list.

Here are the most recent lists as of this book's publication. Visit ewg.org for the current lists or download their mobile app.

DIRTY DOZEN

1. Apples
2. Strawberries
3. Grapes
4. Celery
5. Peaches
6. Spinach
7. Sweet bell peppers
8. Nectarines (imported)
9. Cucumbers
10. Potatoes
11. Cherry tomatoes
12. Chile peppers

CLEAN FIFTEEN

1. Sweet corn
2. Onions
3. Pineapple
4. Avocados
5. Cabbage
6. Sweet peas (frozen)
7. Papayas
8. Mangoes
9. Asparagus
10. Eggplant
11. Kiwis
12. Grapefruit
13. Cantaloupe
14. Sweet potatoes
15. Mushrooms

Caesar in a Glass

My kids refer to this all-vegetable juice as "Caesar salad in a cup." Although it doesn't share many ingredients with the famed salad, it does indeed evoke the zesty flavor of a Caesar. Leave out the garlic, if you like, to make it more like a garden salad instead.

MAKES 15 TO 20 OUNCES

6 medium carrots

1 medium zucchini

1 Roma tomato

1 (2-inch) chunk cucumber

1 garlic clove

1 Trim the carrots and zucchini. Core the tomato.

2 Juice the carrots, zucchini, tomato, cucumber, and garlic according to the directions on your juicing machine. Whisk to combine.

3 Add water to taste if you or your children prefer a milder juice.

Super-Simple Smoothies

Smoothies are sweet, frosty, smooth, and creamy, perfect for a hot summer day. They can serve as a quick breakfast on the go, and they're a simple, fun treat for kids.

But you might hesitate after reading the ingredient lists of commercially produced smoothies. Smoothie bars and many home smoothie recipes rely on frozen yogurt, ice cream, sherbet, or sorbet to add sweetness and body. Those smoothies are really dessert in disguise!

Although I have been known to feed my kids pie and cookies for breakfast on occasion, you and I both know that dessert for breakfast is probably not the best option. Instead, I propose a round of smoothies made with fresh or frozen fruit, unsweetened yogurt, milk or coconut milk, natural sweeteners, and crushed ice. These smoothies are just as satisfying as their ultra-rich counterparts but far more nutritious.

The smoothie recipes that follow are each designed to serve one. If you'd like to make more than one serving, simply double or triple the recipe as desired.

Strawberry Colada

Pineapple and coconut are a classic combination. Add some strawberries for color and you've got a kid-favorite smoothie that will leave them as pleased as punch. Allow the frozen strawberries to thaw just a bit before blending. This will help prevent those big icy chunks that sometimes get left behind at the bottom of the glass. If your strawberries aren't super sweet, add a little honey syrup to taste.

The crushed ice makes for a frosty treat with a texture like that of soft-serve ice cream. Leave out the ice for a thinner, drinkable concoction.

SERVES 1

1 cup frozen strawberries

½ cup pineapple chunks

½ cup canned light coconut milk

½ cup crushed ice (optional)

Honey Syrup (page 154) to taste (optional)

1 Place the strawberries, pineapple, coconut milk, and crushed ice, if using, in the blender cup or pitcher.

2 Blend until very smooth.

3 Adjust for sweetness by adding honey syrup to taste.

Tropical Freeze

This smoothie, blended with the flavors of the tropics, is cool and refreshing. Use freshly squeezed orange juice if possible; bottled pineapple juice is fine. The powdered milk adds protein and creamy goodness without watering down the drink.

SERVES 1

1 cup crushed ice

½ cup orange juice

½ cup pineapple juice

1 small banana, broken into chunks

1 tablespoon nonfat dry milk powder

1 Place the ice, orange juice, pineapple juice, banana, and milk powder in the blender cup or pitcher.

2 Blend until very smooth.

Banana-Cherry-Pom Smoothie

FishBoy13 has been wary of bananas since he was a toddler, shying away from them even in smoothie form. I have no idea why. Maybe I fed him too many bananas as a baby? But this smoothie, tart and sweet from the cherries, berries, and pomegranate juice, convinced him to give bananas another try.

SERVES 1

1 small banana, broken into chunks

½ cup pomegranate juice

½ cup crushed ice

½ cup frozen cherries or cherry-berry mixed fruit

1 Place the banana, pomegranate juice, ice, and frozen fruit in the blender cup or pitcher.

2 Blend until very smooth.

Blueberry-Banana-Coconut Blender

Canned light coconut milk is a useful item to keep on hand in your pantry. It's an ideal substitute for regular milk, offering a shelf-stable alternative to dairy. Try to find a variety without added ingredients. The blueberries and banana in this smoothie add sweetness, antioxidants, and a good dose of potassium.

SERVES 1

1 cup fresh or frozen blueberries

1 small banana, broken into chunks

½ cup crushed ice

½ cup canned light coconut milk

1   Place the blueberries, banana, ice, and coconut milk in the blender cup or pitcher.

2   Blend until very smooth.

Super-Simple Smoothies

Peaches 'n' Cream Yogurt Smoothie

My kids love drinkable yogurts or flavored kefir. This peaches-and-cream-flavored smoothie reminds them of the beverages they love but doesn't give me sticker shock. If your peach is particularly sweet, you can omit the honey syrup.

SERVES 1

1 medium peach, sliced and frozen, or 1 cup frozen peach slices

½ cup plain yogurt

¼ cup milk

1 tablespoon Honey Syrup (page 154)

¼ teaspoon pure vanilla extract

1   Place the peach slices, yogurt, milk, honey syrup, and vanilla extract in the blender cup or pitcher.

2   Blend until very smooth.

Orange Cream Smoothie

When I was a child, a trip to the mall invariably ended with my pleading for an Orange Julius. That cold, creamy orange frothiness in a cup was a delightfully sweet treat. When I achieved this near replica at home, I literally shouted with joy. It tasted just like I remembered.

When I approached my husband with a sample, he protested, "But I don't like Orange Julius." He tasted it anyway—and proceeded to drain the glass, saying, "I guess I like Orange Julius now." The kids, of course, followed suit. You can use either freshly squeezed orange juice or the bottled or concentrate variety.

SERVES 1

1 cup orange juice

1 cup crushed ice

2 tablespoons Honey Syrup (page 154)

1 tablespoon nonfat dry milk powder

¼ teaspoon pure vanilla extract

1 Place the orange juice, ice, honey syrup, milk powder, and vanilla extract in the blender cup or pitcher.

2 Blend until very smooth.

Make a Juice, Make a Smoothie?

When do you make something into a juice? And when do you make a smoothie? One major difference between the two is that smoothies contain fiber and juices do not. There's a great debate about which is best for you, and both sides have valid points. Juicing fans say that we maximize our intake of vitamins and minerals by drinking juice without the fiber. (And studies have shown that consuming reasonable quantities of juice will not cause tooth decay or weight gain, as some have suggested.) Smoothie fans, on the other hand, root for including fiber to aid healthy digestion.

Consider the fruit or vegetables you have on hand. What sounds good today?

JUICE IT ALL.

Almost any fruit or vegetable can be juiced, with the exception of bananas and avocados. Since they are so soft, pulpy, and "creamy," those are best left for smoothies.

USE THE SOFT IN SMOOTHIES.

Soft fruits and vegetables, like berries, bananas, stone fruit, pineapple, mangoes, kale, spinach, and avocados will puree easily in the blender, making them ideal candidates for smoothies. But very hard fruits and vegetables, like apples, carrots, or uncooked sweet potatoes, won't easily or quickly blend to a smooth consistency in a standard blender. Save those for juicing, or use them lightly cooked.

Spiced Banana-Coconut Lassi

Kids love it when you share tastes from other cultures; it makes them feel cosmopolitan. A *lassi* is a cooling yogurt drink popular in India. This one, featuring banana, coconut milk, and baking spices, is sure to please.

SERVES 1

1 cup crushed ice

½ cup canned light coconut milk

½ cup plain yogurt

1 small banana, broken into chunks

2 tablespoons Honey Syrup (page 154)

⅛ teaspoon ground cinnamon

Pinch of ground cardamom

1 Place the ice, coconut milk, yogurt, banana, honey syrup, cinnamon, and cardamom in the blender cup or pitcher.

2 Blend until very smooth.

Pumpkin Spice Smoothie

Here's a smoothie that would please Harry Potter and his friends. My kids can name all the houses of Hogwarts as well as list the various foods and drinks (like pumpkin juice!) served up in the dining room. This smoothie, which FishBoy9 calls "pumpkin pie in a glass," would fit right in with the Hogwarts menu. Canned pumpkin is both a convenient and a nutrient-dense food, a great source of vitamins A and C.

SERVES 1

1 cup crushed ice

¾ cup whole milk

¼ cup canned pumpkin puree (not pumpkin pie mix)

2 tablespoons pure maple syrup

¼ teaspoon pure vanilla extract

⅛ teaspoon ground cinnamon

⅛ teaspoon ground nutmeg

⅛ teaspoon ground ginger

1   Place the ice, milk, pumpkin puree, maple syrup, vanilla extract, cinnamon, nutmeg, and ginger in the blender cup or pitcher.

2   Blend until very smooth.

The Blue Orange

When I was a new mom living in Santa Barbara, I went on daily walks, pushing the baby stroller down the road to the local smoothie bar, where the menu boasted items with names like the Red Banana and the Blue Orange. A midday smoothie was a filling, nutrient-rich snack that fueled the both of us. Although we no longer live in that neighborhood, we visit there often and treat the kids to their favorite smoothies. And we enjoy our own versions at home. This is my re-creation of the Blue Orange. You can use either freshly squeezed OJ or the bottled or concentrate variety.

SERVES 1

½ cup orange juice

½ cup frozen strawberries

½ cup frozen blueberries

½ cup plain yogurt

Honey Syrup (page 154) to taste (optional)

1 Place the orange juice, strawberries, blueberries, and yogurt in the blender cup or pitcher.

2 Blend until very smooth.

3 Adjust for sweetness by adding honey syrup to taste, if desired.

Sweet! And How to Make It So, Naturally

"We elves try to stick to the four main food groups:
candy, candy canes, candy corns, and syrup."
—BUDDY THE ELF, FROM THE FILM *ELF*

In *Elf*, Buddy, a human raised by elves, explains that the elves' diet consists mainly of sugar. That may be okay if you live with Santa at the North Pole, but it's not the best of regimens for the rest of us.

The more sugar we eat, the more we crave. It's a hard habit to break. I've experimented with sugar-free eating and found that abstaining from sugar increases my alertness and improves my general well being.

Weaning ourselves from processed sugars can have a positive effect on the whole family. Who hasn't seen kids too amped up on sweets? A sugar overdose can wreak havoc on the happiest of holidays or the most mundane of weekdays.

I've found that it helps my family if we reduce our processed sugars and look to nature's candy—fruit and a bit of honey—to sweeten our treats. The juices in this book are made entirely from fruits, vegetables, herbs, and spices, while some of the sports drinks, smoothies, sodas, slushies, and ice pops get a little boost from real maple syrup or one of the following honey syrups.

Honey Syrup

Honey Syrup is easy to make, stores well for at least a week in the refrigerator, and mixes easily into cold drinks. Keep it on hand to flavor the fun drinks in this book and to sweeten your iced tea or coffee.

MAKES 2 CUPS

1 cup honey
1 cup water

1 Combine the honey and water in a medium saucepan.

2 Bring to a simmer over medium heat, stirring to dissolve the honey completely.

3 Remove from the heat and let cool completely.

4 Store in a covered container in the refrigerator.

Ginger Honey Syrup

This ginger-flavored honey mixture is the key component of homemade ginger ale (page 181); it's also a delicate sweetener for sports drinks and other beverages, and it works well in hot or iced black or green tea.

MAKES 2 CUPS

1 cup honey

1 cup water

¼ cup finely chopped peeled fresh ginger

1. Combine the honey, water, and ginger in a medium saucepan.

2. Bring to a simmer over medium heat, stirring to dissolve the honey completely.

3. Simmer for 30 minutes.

4. Strain the liquid through a fine-mesh strainer, discarding the solids. Let cool completely.

5. Store in a covered container in the refrigerator.

Mint Honey Syrup

Mint has a cooling, relaxing effect, and this syrup is delicious in a number of beverages. It's a favorite in tea and coffee drinks as well as in homemade sodas and sports drinks.

MAKES 2 CUPS

1 cup honey

1 cup water

¾ cup finely chopped fresh mint leaves

1. Combine the honey, water, and mint in a medium saucepan.

2. Bring to a simmer over medium heat, stirring to dissolve the honey completely.

3. Simmer for 30 minutes.

4. Strain the liquid through a fine-mesh strainer, discarding the solids. Let cool completely.

5. Store in a covered container in the refrigerator.

Blueberry Fields Blender

This is what I call a stealth smoothie. My kids have no idea it's chock full of greens. Use a mixture of baby greens, or chop up whatever greens you have on hand: spinach, chard, or kale. The blueberries and honey syrup add a fruity sweetness that disguises the vegetables.

SERVES 1

1 cup crushed ice

1 cup fresh or frozen blueberries

1 cup chopped greens (such as baby greens, spinach, chard, kale, or a mixture)

½ cup canned light coconut milk

1 tablespoon Honey Syrup (page 154), or more to taste

1 Place the ice, blueberries, greens, coconut milk, and honey syrup in the blender cup or pitcher.

2 Blend until very smooth.

3 Adjust for sweetness by adding more honey syrup, if desired.

Chocolate-Banana-Coco Smoothie

Years ago, fresh out of high school, I sold frozen chocolate-dipped bananas at a Los Angeles amusement park. It was a fun summer: most of my customers truly wanted to be there, and the festive atmosphere of roller coasters, carnival games, and fun food was always a thrill. Steady business at the banana cart taught me that the combination of chocolate and banana is always popular. This smoothie further proves the point.

SERVES 1

1 cup crushed ice

1 small banana, broken into chunks

½ cup canned light coconut milk

1 tablespoon natural unsweetened cocoa powder

1 tablespoon Honey Syrup (page 154), or more to taste

1 Place the ice, banana, coconut milk, cocoa powder, and honey syrup in the blender cup or pitcher.

2 Blend until very smooth.

3 Adjust for sweetness by adding more honey syrup, if desired.

Chocolate & Banana Nut Butter Blast

The classic combination of bananas and peanut butter is reworked in this smoothie. The banana contributes potassium and fiber, and the nut or seed butter adds protein. The chocolate makes it a little more "fun," but feel free to make it without the cocoa powder if you or your kids prefer.

SERVES 1

1 cup crushed ice

1 small banana, broken into chunks

½ cup milk

1 tablespoon natural unsweetened cocoa powder

1 tablespoon peanut butter or other nut or seed butter of your choice

1 Place the ice, banana, milk, cocoa powder, and nut or seed butter in the blender cup or pitcher.

2 Blend until very smooth.

Smoothie Success

ON INGREDIENTS: I've found that crushed ice works well for making smooth smoothies in a standard blender, leaving no big chunks of ice cube to wrangle with at the bottom of the cup. If your refrigerator's icemaker doesn't have a crushed-ice option, simply place several ice cubes in a zip-top freezer bag and pound it a few times with a kitchen mallet to break up the cubes.

Some varieties of fruit, like strawberries or bananas, may be a little resistant to smooth blending when frozen. Allow these items to thaw for a few minutes before blending to achieve a smoother texture.

Feel free to boost your smoothies with other ingredients, such as flax seeds, chia seeds, protein powder, or dry powdered milk. Chopped leafy greens practically disappear in smoothies, boosting their nutrition while leaving children none the wiser.

ON BLENDERS: Our family uses a blender with individual "party cups." These are individual mugs that fit onto the blender base. Thanks to these handy cups, every kid can have a different flavor when I make smoothies. I don't have to make a whole pitcher and hear the inevitable "But I don't want that kind." This way, too, I don't have to wash a large blender and all the separate serving cups. With the party cups, I can serve in the blending vessel itself.

If you don't already have this type of blender, you don't need to make a special purchase. Standard Mason jars fit a standard blender base, allowing you to use them as party cups.

And of course, those of you with high-speed, smoothie-bar-quality blenders will find making smoothies a super-simple affair, with or without the party cups.

ON MAKING SMOOTHIES AHEAD: Smoothies are very freezer friendly. You can make a bulk batch and freeze the smoothies in individual containers with lids. They will thaw quickly on the counter, making for easy on-the-go breakfasts and snacks.

ON MAKING IT SELF-SERVE: We have set up the bottom drawer of our freezer as a DIY smoothie station. There, my kids can find a variety of frozen fruit. I freeze dollops of plain yogurt on a plastic-lined baking sheet. Once those are frozen, I collect them in a zip-top freezer bag and store the bag in the smoothie station. Family members can then create their own custom smoothies whenever they want, since they know where to find all the ingredients.

ON WASTING LESS: Smoothies are typically based on fruits and dairy. These are items that can spoil if not used in a timely fashion. Freeze a surplus of fruit and enjoy it later in smoothies. Bananas, peaches, and berries freeze well without any special treatment. Place washed berries or peeled and sliced bananas or peaches on a lined baking sheet and place the sheet in the freezer. Once the fruit is frozen, place it in a zip-top freezer bag, and store the bag in the freezer.

The same can be done for dairy items like milk or yogurt. Freeze either in ice cube trays. Thicker yogurts can be dropped in dollops onto a plastic-lined baking sheet and placed in the freezer. Once the cubes or dollops are frozen, place them in a labeled, zip-top freezer bag and store the bag in the freezer.

Ice-Blended Milk Nog

My kids love the commercial eggnog and milk nog that are available in winter. This homemade alternative is delicious any time of year. I call for whole milk here; you can use lower-fat milk, but the drink won't be as creamy or nog-like. Want to make this more of a dessert? Substitute whipping cream for some of the milk.

SERVES 1

1 cup crushed ice

¾ cup whole milk

1 tablespoon pure maple syrup

¼ teaspoon pure vanilla extract

⅛ teaspoon ground cinnamon

⅛ teaspoon ground nutmeg

1 Place the ice, milk, maple syrup, vanilla extract, cinnamon, and nutmeg in the blender cup or pitcher.

2 Blend until very smooth.

Spiffy Sports Drinks, Sparklies, Slushies & Ice Pops

Chances are you've heard your kids' pleas for bottled sports drinks, canned sodas, convenience store slushies, or ice pops from the ice cream truck. I want to say, "Yes!" Who doesn't want to be a "Yes Mom"? I cringe, however, at both the cost and the quality of these processed treats.

But no longer!

With a blender, a supply of fun cups and straws, ice pop molds, and a few bottles of soda water, I can be the coolest mom on the block. These treats are tasty, naturally sweetened, and sure to please kids of all ages.

Once you start making your own, you won't want to go back to commercial sweet treats.

SPORTS DRINKS

SPARKLIES

SLUSHIES

ICE POPS

SPORTS DRINKS

Three of my sons play inline hockey. With weekly practices and games, they're perspiring and in the process losing precious salts and minerals that sports drinks are designed to replace. Although a bottled sports drink can quench the thirst and replenish nutrients, it may also be filled with dubious ingredients and too much sweetener.

The following sports drinks and ades fit the bill without emptying the pocketbook. Naturally sweetened with honey syrup, they are designed to re-energize and rehydrate without weighing a kid down when he wants to get back in the game.

These beverages aren't just for sports, though. They can bring refreshment on a hot day and wholesome comfort to someone laid up in bed with a cold or stomach bug.

Grape Sports Ade

This thirst quencher comes together quickly with bottled grape juice. My tasters say it far surpasses the store-bought versions.

MAKES 1 QUART

3¼ cups water

½ cup grape juice

⅓ cup Honey Syrup (page 154)

¼ teaspoon fine sea salt

1 In a pitcher, whisk together the water, grape juice, honey syrup, and salt.

2 Store in a covered jar or container in the refrigerator. Serve chilled.

Orange Sports Ade

Although my kids are familiar with commercial sports drinks bearing names like Orange Lightning Rain or Purple Mega Zephyr, my husband and I grew up in an era when there were two choices: lemon-lime and orange. He prefers orange. This is a more healthful version of what you might buy in a store. It tastes best with freshly squeezed orange juice, but it can certainly be made with bottled.

MAKES 1 QUART

3 cups water

1 cup orange juice

¼ cup Ginger Honey Syrup (page 155)

¼ teaspoon fine sea salt

1 In a pitcher, whisk together the water, orange juice, honey syrup, and salt.

2 Store in a covered jar or container in the refrigerator. Serve chilled.

Lemon-Lime Sports Ade

This lemon-lime drink tastes like the bottled or powdered version I enjoyed as a child. Inexpensive to mix up, it's delightfully refreshing. Use freshly squeezed juices for the best flavor. Feel free to use one of the flavored honey syrups on page 155 if you prefer a twist of ginger or mint.

MAKES 1 QUART

3½ cups water

6 tablespoons Honey Syrup (page 154)

2 tablespoons freshly squeezed lemon juice

2 tablespoons freshly squeezed lime juice

¼ teaspoon fine sea salt

1 In a pitcher, whisk together the water, honey syrup, lemon and lime juices, and salt.

2 Store in a covered jar or container in the refrigerator. Serve chilled.

Coco-Loco Sports Drink

This drink is a big hit with my kids, disappearing in a flash whenever I serve it. Flavored with pineapple juice and coconut water, it features the flavors of the tropics. Coconut water is naturally rich in potassium, making it a great post-workout drink. Feel free to use bottled or canned pineapple juice if it's more convenient.

MAKES 1 QUART

1 (17.5-ounce) can or carton coconut water

1¾ cups water

½ cup pineapple juice

2 tablespoons Honey Syrup (page 154)

¼ teaspoon fine sea salt

1 In a pitcher, whisk together the coconut water, water, pineapple juice, honey syrup, and salt.

2 Store in a covered jar or container in the refrigerator. Serve chilled.

Green Tea Sports Drink

Green tea is packed with antioxidants, which can boost the immune system and help prevent or treat flu and colds. It's considered safe for children, though it's not recommended for babies and toddlers. Green tea has a small amount of caffeine (less than many bottled sodas!), but if you are concerned, it is also available in a decaffeinated version; either one makes a good base for a sports drink. If your kids aren't regular tea drinkers, they may need to try it a few times to become accustomed to the taste. For a lighter tea flavor, simply use less tea and more water. Thanks to the Wellness Mama blog for the inspiration to try green tea in a sports drink.

MAKES 1 QUART

2 cups brewed green tea, chilled

1½ cups water

¼ cup Ginger Honey Syrup (page 155)

2 tablespoons freshly squeezed lemon juice

¼ teaspoon fine sea salt

1 In a pitcher, whisk together the tea, water, honey syrup, lemon juice, and salt.

2 Store in a covered jar or container in the refrigerator. Serve chilled.

Ma's Ginger Water

Fans of the Laura Ingalls Wilder Little House books may remember when Ma mixed up a jug of vinegar, ginger, honey, and water for the girls to take to Pa out in the field. They called it "ginger water." This traditional ade, often called switchel or haymaker's punch, was mixed up by farm wives across the prairie as a thirst quencher for the crews working in the field. This version has a unique and refreshing flavor.

MAKES ABOUT 1 QUART

4 cups water

6 tablespoons Ginger Honey Syrup (page 155)

2 tablespoons apple cider vinegar

¼ teaspoon fine sea salt

1   In a pitcher, whisk together the water, honey syrup, vinegar, and salt.

2   Store in a covered jar or container in the refrigerator. Serve chilled.

Pink Lemonade Zephyr

I couldn't resist giving this a goofy name, especially since it's not really a lemonade. It's a sports drink. May it make you as swift as the wind! Bottled pomegranate juice makes it easy to put together and gives it great flavor and a punch of nutritious goodness. Use ginger or plain honey syrup, depending on your preference.

MAKES 1 QUART

3 cups water

⅓ cup Honey Syrup (page 154) or Ginger Honey Syrup (page 155)

¼ cup pomegranate juice

2 tablespoons freshly squeezed lemon juice

¼ teaspoon fine sea salt

1   In a pitcher, whisk together the water, honey syrup, pomegranate and lemon juices, and salt.

2   Store in a covered jar or container in the refrigerator. Serve chilled.

Watermelon Cool

Watermelon and mint are natural partners, offering a tasty way to cool off on a hot day. Run a few chunks of watermelon through the juice extractor prior to whipping this up. This sweet drink is a favorite with all the kids in my neighborhood. Make it, and you'll be the "Cool Ade Mom," for sure.

MAKES 1 QUART

2⅔ cups water

1 cup watermelon juice (from 2 cups of 1-inch watermelon cubes, juiced in the juice extractor)

¼ to ⅓ cup Mint Honey Syrup (page 155), or to taste

¼ teaspoon fine sea salt

1 In a pitcher, whisk together the water, watermelon juice, honey syrup, and salt.

2 Store in a covered jar or container in the refrigerator. Serve chilled.

SPARKLIES

At our house, the word "sparklies" refers to any drink with bubbles or carbonation. For instance, sparkling apple cider is known as "apple sparkly." At the holidays, I've mixed cranberry juice concentrate with soda water for—you guessed it—"cranberry sparkly." Since we no longer drink soda pop on a regular basis, homemade sparklies have taken center stage.

With a few jars of flavored honey syrups in the fridge and a supply of soda water in the pantry, you can make refreshing treats whenever you like.

Lime-Mint Cooler

The Cubans had the right idea when they combined lime and mint flavors in their national cocktail. This lime-mint cooler is a kid-friendly version of the mojito. It's light and refreshing, like summer and happiness all in one glass.

SERVES 1

¼ cup Mint Honey Syrup (page 155)
2 tablespoons freshly squeezed lime juice
1 cup chilled club soda

1   Pour the honey syrup and lime juice into a tall glass filled with ice.

2   Add the soda water and stir gently to combine. Serve immediately.

Mock Orangina

I lived in France for a year during college. It was there that I met the sweet-tart orange-flavored soda that is popular in Europe. This do-it-yourself version, a mixture of freshly squeezed citrus juices, is refreshing and fun. Your kids will be thrilled with homemade orange soda.

MAKES ABOUT 5 CUPS

1½ cups freshly squeezed orange juice (from 6 or 7 medium oranges)

½ cup freshly squeezed lemon juice (from about 3 lemons)

½ cup freshly squeezed mandarin orange juice (from 4 or 5 mandarin oranges)

¼ cup Honey Syrup (page 154), or to taste

2 cups chilled soda water

1 In a pitcher, whisk together the orange, lemon, and mandarin orange juices and honey syrup. Chill.

2 Just before serving, add the soda water. Serve over ice.

Cactus Coolio

Once upon a time, a guy named Fred Flintstone loved a drink called Cactus Cooler. I dressed up as Fred for Halloween when I was five. True story. There were no other costumes to choose from by the time my dad took me to the drugstore. I was Fred— with pigtails.

Years later, in junior high, I favored a soda by the same name. This pineapple-orange concoction is reminiscent of that cool can of refreshment that I could buy from the vending machine—only this is cheaper and more nutritious. For the best flavor, use freshly squeezed orange juice, but canned pineapple juice is fine.

MAKES ABOUT 1 QUART

1 cup freshly squeezed orange juice (from about 4 oranges)

1 cup pineapple juice

½ cup Honey Syrup (page 154)

2 cups soda water

1   In a pitcher, whisk together the orange and pineapple juices and honey syrup. Chill.

2   Just before serving, add the soda water. Serve over ice.

Homemade Honey Ginger Ale

Ginger ale has always been one of my comfort drinks, whether as a childhood treat or a mainstay in the early days of pregnancy. My family and I enjoy sipping this homemade version on pizza night or when the occasional tummy bug hits. Keep a jar of Ginger Honey Syrup on hand in order to mix up a glass of homemade ginger ale any time.

SERVES 1

3 tablespoons Ginger Honey Syrup (page 155)
1 cup chilled soda water

1   Pour the honey syrup into a tall glass filled with ice.

2   Add the soda water and stir gently to combine. Serve immediately.

Spiffy
Sports
Drinks,
Sparklies,
Slushies, &
Ice Pops

181

SLUSHIES

Remember riding your bike down to the corner convenience store for a great big frosty slushie or Slurpee? I do. That sweet, icy goodness was hard to resist, even though it inevitably resulted in a brain freeze from slurping it down a little too quickly.

Nowadays, a wholesome homemade slushie is just minutes away as long as I have frozen fruit or juice, honey syrup, and crushed ice at the ready. Crushed ice works better in the blender than cubes. You'll achieve that slushie consistency more quickly and easily.

Strawberry Agua Fresca

An *agua fresca*—Spanish for "fresh water"—is a popular fruit drink in Mexico and Central America. It is cool and refreshing, often flavored with fruit and lime or lemon juice.

SERVES 2

2 cups sliced strawberries

2 tablespoons freshly squeezed lime juice

¼ cup Honey Syrup (page 154), or more to taste

1 cup cold water

1 Place the strawberries, lime juice, honey syrup, and a little of the water in a blender. Blend to a smooth consistency.

2 Stir in the remaining cold water.

3 Serve immediately.

Frozen Pomegranate Lemonade

This sweet-tart slushie comes together quickly in the blender. You can use bottled pomegranate juice for convenience, but freshly squeezed lemon juice will add great flavor.

SERVES 1

> 1 cup crushed ice
>
> ½ cup pomegranate juice
>
> 3 tablespoons Honey Syrup (page 154)
>
> 2 tablespoons freshly squeezed lemon juice

1 Place the ice, pomegranate juice, honey syrup, and lemon juice in the blender. Blend on medium to high speed until well mixed and smooth.

2 Serve immediately.

Every Berry Slushie

This fruit-based slushie relies on frozen fruit to give it flavor and texture. Use your favorite blend of mixed berries. Or if you'd prefer, choose a single berry. This bulk batch is sure to be a hit with your crowd. It is with mine.

SERVES 4

2 cups mixed frozen berries

2 cups cold water

¾ cup crushed ice

¼ cup Honey Syrup (page 154)

1 Place the berries, water, ice, and honey syrup in the blender. Blend on medium to high speed until well mixed and smooth.

2 Serve immediately.

ICE POPS

Ice pops are a surefire hit with my crew on warm spring days, hot summer nights, and, well, any time. I've yet to meet a kid who will turn down a frozen pop.

They are also welcome comforts when the kids have fevers or upset tummies. Sucking on an ice pop allows for slow rehydration—important during and after bouts of stomach trouble. And mamas in labor can benefit from a tasty ice pop as well. My nurse in labor and delivery offered them to me to give me stamina for that physical journey into motherhood.

Ice Pop Molds

One of the keys to making ice pops is finding the right molds. Some cheaper plastic molds just don't work. How disappointing when the frozen ice pop stays behind in the mold while the stick pulls clean out!

Often this is because the plastic stick has no holes in it! Good old-fashioned wooden popsicle sticks are porous and expand in water, so the liquid adheres to the stick as it freezes. Good quality plastic ice pop molds will have holes in the stick so that the liquid freezes through the stick and holds firm.

Look for BPA-free molds with wooden sticks or plastic sticks with several holes in them. My husband retrofitted an inexpensive set we had by drilling three holes through each stick.

Remember, too, that you can also make ice pops without a special mold. Use small paper or plastic cups with flat wooden spoons, wooden craft sticks, or regular wooden ice pop sticks. If the liquid is not thick enough to hold the stick upright, you can do one of two things:

1 Cover the cup with plastic wrap and cut a small hole for the stick to slide through.

2 Allow the liquid to freeze slightly, and add the stick as soon as the liquid can hold it upright.

Strawberries & Cream Yogurt Ice Pops

The sweetness of these ice pops will vary, depending on the sweetness of your strawberries. Since the yogurt is unsweetened, you could end up with a very tart pop. Add more honey syrup if your strawberries aren't quite the sweetest of the season. Add less, to taste, if you've found berries at their peak.

MAKES ABOUT 2 CUPS ICE POP MIXTURE

2 cups stemmed, sliced strawberries

½ cup plain yogurt

¼ cup Honey Syrup (page 154)

½ teaspoon pure vanilla extract

1 Combine the strawberries, yogurt, honey syrup, and vanilla extract in a blender or a food processor fitted with a metal blade. Blend until the mixture is very smooth.

2 Pour into ice pop molds and freeze.

3 Remove the frozen ice pops from the molds and serve. You may need to hold the molds under warm water for a moment to thaw the pops slightly and loosen them from the molds.

Ginger-Lemon Ice Pops

These pops, flavored with ginger, lemon, and honey, are refreshing on a hot day, but they are also extra soothing for sore throats. A source of vitamin C and antioxidants, they make a perfect pick-me-up. Use freshly squeezed lemon juice for best flavor.

MAKES ABOUT 2 CUPS ICE POP MIXTURE

2 cups water

½ cup freshly squeezed lemon juice

½ cup Ginger Honey Syrup (page 155)

1 Whisk together the water, lemon juice, and syrup in a pitcher.

2 Pour into ice pop molds and freeze.

3 Remove the frozen ice pops from the molds and serve. You may need to hold the molds under warm water for a moment to thaw the pops slightly and loosen them from the molds.

Coconut-Pineapple Paletas

Years ago, my husband and I went on a mission trip to Honduras, staying with a local family to experience the culture firsthand. Hermana Elena made *paletas,* sweet ice pops in different flavors. Everyone in our travel group loved the pops. This version is sure to please kids of all ages. Fresh pineapple is nice here, but for convenience's sake, feel free to use canned pineapple.

MAKES ABOUT 2 CUPS ICE POP MIXTURE

2 cups pineapple cubes

1 cup canned light coconut milk

1 tablespoon Honey Syrup (page 154)

1 Combine the pineapple, coconut milk, and honey syrup in a blender or a food processor fitted with a metal blade. Blend until the mixture is fairly smooth. It's okay to leave little bits of pineapple.

2 Pour into ice pop molds and freeze.

3 Remove the frozen ice pops from the molds and serve. You may need to hold the molds under warm water for a moment to thaw the pops slightly and loosen them from the molds.

Banana Fudge Ice Pops

Recipes for chocolate and banana "ice cream" have circulated for years. These fudge pops borrow from those flavors and textures. For best results, slice the bananas ahead of time and freeze them for a few hours before blending.

MAKES ABOUT 2 CUPS ICE POP MIXTURE

2 bananas, sliced and frozen

1¼ cups milk

3 tablespoons natural unsweetened cocoa powder

1 tablespoon pure maple syrup

1 teaspoon pure vanilla extract

1 teaspoon ground cinnamon

Pinch of salt

1   Combine the bananas, milk, cocoa powder, maple syrup, vanilla extract, cinnamon, and salt in a blender or a food processor fitted with a metal blade. Blend until the mixture is very smooth.

2   Pour into ice pop molds and freeze.

3   Remove the frozen ice pops from the molds and serve. You may need to hold the molds under warm water for a moment to thaw the pops slightly and loosen them from the molds.

Spiffy
Sports
Drinks,
Sparklies,
Slushies, &
Ice Pops

191

Yogurt-Peach Ice Pops

These layered ice pops take a few more steps to prepare than the other ice pops, but they are quite the novelty. Who doesn't like layers of flavors and colors? Feel free to make layered pops with other fruit purees, adjusting the sweetener to taste.

MAKES ABOUT 2 CUPS ICE POP MIXTURE

> 2 peaches, peeled, halved and pitted (or one 15-ounce can peaches in juice, drained)
>
> ¼ cup Honey Syrup (page 154)
>
> 1 tablespoon freshly squeezed lemon juice
>
> ½ cup plain yogurt
>
> 1 tablespoon honey

1 Place the peaches, honey syrup, and lemon juice in a blender or a food processor fitted with a metal blade. Blend until the mixture is very smooth.

2 In a small bowl, combine the yogurt and honey. Stir until well combined.

3 Pour half of the peach mixture into ice pop molds. Make a second layer, using the yogurt mixture. Top with a layer of the remaining peach mixture. Freeze until firm.

4 Remove the frozen ice pops from the molds and serve. You may need to hold the molds under warm water for a moment to thaw the pops slightly and loosen them from the molds.

Acknowledgments

This book has been an adventure of fresh fruit and vegetables and equally fresh responses when one of my sweet children didn't care for a particular juice we were testing. ("This one tastes like wood!") It's been fun and full of laughter. And it's been tasty. Well, except for the woody one.

Many thanks are in order:

Thank you to the team at The Harvard Common Press, whom I consider my East Coast family. What a blessing to work with a group of genuinely kind and courteous people. Thanks to Bruce Shaw for his confidence in me, this simple home cook; to Adam Salomone for his enthusiasm and creativity—and for always laughing at my jokes; to Dan Rosenberg for his wise guidance throughout it all; and to Valerie Cimino and Jane Dornbusch, the only people in the world who can make me view red correcting marks as the kisses of friends. Thank you, Pat Jalbert-Levine, for your amazing attention to detail; and thank you to the creative team: designer Laura Palese, photographer Brian Samuels, and production manager Virginia Downes.

Big thanks to my agent, Alison Picard, for her steadfast confidence in my abilities and for creating a match made in heaven by connecting me with The Harvard Common Press.

Thank you to my blog readers at Life as Mom and Good Cheap Eats. Your enthusiasm and support of my recipes and writing are fuel to a sometimes-weary heart. Thanks to friends and family who offered input and served as taste testers, including but not limited to: Alice, Bethany, Debbie, Jessika, Lynn, Michelle, Sharon, Sheila, Stacy, Stephanie, and the Bechler family. Thank you, Mom, Dad, Jamie, Janel, John, and Jace; I imagine you're used to my crazy ways by now. Thanks for putting up with me.

Special thanks to my six precious children, who willingly drank any and every juice I handed them. Thank you for giving me honest yet witty feedback. I can't wait to see where God takes you in life. Thank you for embracing your mama's projects so willingly. You make my life so very rich.

Deep gratitude goes to my sweet husband, who has encouraged and cajoled me, solved problems with and for me, and so happily embraced this recipe-testing, cookbook-writing, blog-posting life. The last 20 years have been better than I ever guessed they would be. Here's to a lifetime of more.

My ultimate thanks to Jesus, who has given me all good things.

Measurement Equivalents

Please note that all conversions are approximate.

Liquid Conversions

U.S.	Metric
1 tsp	5 ml
1 tbs	15 ml
2 tbs	30 ml
3 tbs	45 ml
¼ cup	60 ml
⅓ cup	75 ml
⅓ cup + 1 tbs	90 ml
⅓ cup + 2 tbs	100 ml
½ cup	120 ml
⅔ cup	150 ml
¾ cup	180 ml
¾ cup + 2 tbs	200 ml
1 cup	240 ml
1 cup + 2 tbs	275 ml
1¼ cups	300 ml
1⅓ cups	325 ml
1½ cups	350 ml
1¾ cups	375 ml
1¾ cups	400 ml
1¾ cups + 2 tbs	450 ml
2 cups (1 pint)	475 ml
2½ cups	600 ml
3 cups	720 ml
4 cups (1 quart)	945 ml
(1,000 ml is 1 liter)	

Weight Conversions

U.S./U.K.	Metric
½ oz	14 g
1 oz	28 g
1½ oz	43 g
2 oz	57 g
2½ oz	71 g
3 oz	85 g
3½ oz	100 g
4 oz	113 g
5 oz	142 g
6 oz	170 g
7 oz	200 g
8 oz	227 g
9 oz	255 g
10 oz	284 g
11 oz	312 g
12 oz	340 g
13 oz	368 g
14 oz	400 g
15 oz	425 g
1 lb	454 g

Oven Temperature Conversions

°F	Gas Mark	°C
250	½	120
275	1	140
300	2	150
325	3	165
350	4	180
375	5	190
400	6	200
425	7	220
450	8	230
475	9	240
500	10	260
550	Broil	290

Index

Note: Page references in *italics* indicate recipe photographs.

About the Author

JESSICA FISHER writes two very popular blogs, Life as Mom and Good Cheap Eats, which have established her as a go-to authority on cooking for a family cheaply, creatively, and nutritiously.

Best 100 Juices for Kids is her second cookbook. Her bestselling first book, *Not Your Mother's Make-Ahead and Freeze Cookbook,* added to her reputation as a cook and writer with a wealth of clever ideas for feeding a family inexpensively and well. A widely cited figure in the world of food blogs and "mom blogs," she also has written online for The Kitchn, Life Your Way, Money Saving Mom, $5 Dinners, and Simple Mom and in print for more than 85 regional parenting publications. Jessica's readers recognize that she walks the talk: She is the mom to, and primary cook for, four young sons and two young daughters. She lives with her husband and children in the San Diego area.